# Breaking Out

The Journey of Transformation
into the Image of Jesus Christ

# Therese Marszalek

AmErica House
Baltimore

First printing

ISBN: 1-59129-289-1
PUBLISHED BY
AMERICA HOUSE BOOK PUBLISHERS
www.publishamerica.com
Baltimore

Printed in the United States of America

Breaking Out is "quick, powerful, and sharp" and is enveloped with scripture to set the captive free. This anointed writing clearly instructs the believer to understand how to walk the path promised by Jesus, "whom the Son sets free is free indeed." Therese has built a bridge for others to cross by teaching through personal experiences. Highly recommended for pressing on!

Lorelei Wilcox, President and Founder
Lord of the Nations Training Center
House of the Lord Ministries
Tum Tum, Washington

The material in Breaking Out is relative and a vital source for Christians to reach their full potential. Therese has captured clear wisdom within the pages and communicates it in a way any believer can grasp. Without reservation, I would recommend Breaking Out for anyone's personal growth!

Pastor Rick Sharkey, Senior Pastor
Spokane Christian Center
Spokane, Washington

Breaking Out is simply spiritual! It is littered with scripture to help maturing Christians found their life on the unchanging Word of Christ. Are you ready to grow? Fasten your seat belts, this is food for the soul!

John S. Moon, Senior Pastor
Global Harvest Church
Chula Vista, California

Breaking Out is a powerful book that will be an asset to the foundations of any new believer's lifestyle. Therese has captured many of the common questions that often plague new believers. With simple, straightforward answers she addresses each one from a strong scriptural viewpoint. Many will be challenged and provoked to develop a deeper relationship with the Lord Jesus. I recommend Breaking Out, not only for new believers, but also as a tool within the local church to help begin a discipleship program for those looking for solid direction in their commitment to the Lord Jesus Christ and His local church.

Lonny Bingle, Senior Pastor
Spokane Faith Center


Therese has cut to the chase in the search for answers to God's plan for us. Why did Jesus have to die on the cross? How do we overcome jealousy, anger or hatred? Where do we find love, hope and encouragement? Therese combines her own experiences and biblical truth to provide direction for the young and mature Christian alike. Do yourself a favor. Read Breaking Out and get ready to ascend to new heights in your walk with the Lord.

Marcia Kyser-Karr
Fellowship Bible Church
Portland, Oregon


Breaking Out is a must read for any believer who desires to live the Christian life to the full. Succinct and to the point application of Scripture will enable followers of Christ to understand how to walk the Christian walk with Jesus Christ victoriously.

Ivan Roberts, Seniors' Pastor
Spokane Christian Center
Spokane, Washington

I dedicate this book to my beloved mother, Carol Preston, who went home to be with the Lord shortly before *Breaking Out* was completed. She demonstrated the love of Jesus throughout her life and showed me, through her example, what being transformed into the image of Jesus Christ really means.

# TABLE OF CONTENTS

# INTRODUCTION

Out of ignorance and lack of discipleship, I spent the first several years of my journey as a born again Christian in spiritual wilderness. It is my passion to share the journey I made from the wilderness to the Promised Land in an effort to help believers – especially new believers – understand their new identity in Christ Jesus.

As a follower of the Lord Jesus Christ, you are predestined to be conformed to His image in true righteousness and holiness. The wondrous transformation into the image of Jesus is not an overnight process, but instead one that requires a lifelong journey of walking hand in hand with God the Father, God the Son and God the Holy Spirit.

Ephesians 4:22-24 says, "You were taught, with regard to your former way of life, to put off your old self, which is being corrupted by its deceitful desires; to be made new in the attitude of your minds; and to put on the new self, created to be like God in true righteousness and holiness."

*Breaking Out* is a tool that will enable you to take off the old self, renew your mind to the plan of God, and to put on the new self God created you to be in Him.

May the Holy Spirit minister healing and hope as you embark on the journey to your destiny in Christ Jesus.

# CHAPTER 1
## Searching For The Answer

My faithful parents accompanied me to church every Sunday morning as a child. Missing Sunday service due to illness or unexpected emergency meant attending a make up service during the week. Certain that God kept strict church attendance records in heaven, I felt a sense of relief knowing I no longer lagged behind on His divine record sheet. I often wondered how many points were accumulated in my heavenly account. Seeing God as a hard master, I feared Him.

Sitting obediently with properly folded hands, I tried to comprehend the religious sermons preached from the pulpit, yet they sounded like a foreign language in my young ears. The repetitiously memorized prayers were meaningless babble to me; I didn't understand the meaning of the words.

Jesus' lifeless body hung on a rugged cross at the front of the sanctuary. Staring at the massive cross, I felt sorry for Jesus and the suffering I imagined Him enduring at His crucifixion. I wondered, *Why did Jesus die? Why was He crucified? Who inflicted such an awful punishment on a man who seemed so nice? Why did they kill Jesus?* I didn't understand.

Throughout adolescence I pondered the afterlife, and wondered what would happen if I died. *Will I simply drift off into an eternal sleep? Is there a heaven? Is there a hell? Which direction will I go when I die? Does God even exist?* Whirling thoughts about the mystery of the afterlife dominated my quiet moments and provoked great restlessness in my innermost being.

Trying to soothe increasing anxiety, I became falsely convinced of my ability to gain entrance to the security of heaven of my own volition. *If I do enough good deeds... if I can just be good enough,*

*I'll make it to heaven,* subliminally played in the background of my mind. Bouts of sinful living followed good deeds though, squelching my confidence in heaven and leaving me hell bound once again.

Gripped with fear, thoughts of the burning flames of hell tormented my mind. Mounting insecurity of my questionable future eternity became unbearable. Wrestling with fear of the unknown, I sought comfort by pushing unsettling thoughts out of my mind. But the unanswered questions haunted me and I continued to wonder.

Suspecting I had failed to meet heaven's requirements, my growing sense of hopelessness left much consternation. Attempting to reason away my confusion, I rehearsed my qualifications. *I've attended church on Sundays; I've completed all of the religious sacraments and ceremonies; I've done everything I'm supposed to do.* Yet the same question replayed, *So why do I feel so lost inside?* I ignorantly continued my journey in spiritual darkness, not realizing I was indeed lost.

Through the confusion of my spiritual ignorance, I mentally wore the label "Christian." *Of course I'm a Christian,* I thought. *After all, I believe in God. I'm a good person.* Little did I know that believing in God and being a good person were not enough to qualify me for righteousness in God's sight.

The outward appearance of happiness and success followed me as a young adult. Painting a picture of the perfect life, I enjoyed solid independence, a prosperous career, a fat bank account, and popularity amongst my peers.

Smiling through a broken heart, I deceived those around me. The convincing outward contentment masked the torment exploding on the inside though. The false illusion fizzled as a dark cloud of anguish surfaced. Enveloped in restlessness, I silently continued my search for the truth.

Increasing awareness of a deep inner emptiness demanded attention. Desperate to fill the empty hole, I recklessly sought peace and happiness through avenues leading to destruction. Filling my heart's gaping hole with alcohol, promiscuity, and materialism brought only short term numbing to my aching heart. All led to more pain; none satisfied my thirst for inner peace.

Recklessly searching for an avenue to fill my heart's abyss, I spiraled deeper into sin until all attempts to find peace expired. Emotionally fatigued when I arrived at the end of myself, I finally turned to the One who patiently waited for my surrender. With an aching heart, I cried out to the God I wasn't certain even existed. "God, if you're real, I want to know you!" echoed into the heavens.

At the threshold of grief, my precious brother Jim unexpectedly arrived at my door. Extending his open hand, he offered a book containing the yet to be discovered treasure I sought. Unaware that my life was steeped in sin and unaware of my search for the truth he held in his hands, Jim didn't know he was partaking in a God-ordained mission. God had, in fact, heard the cry of my heart.

Out of desperation and a touch of curiosity, I closed myself in my bedroom to read the entire book. My world stood still as I poured through TL Osborne's *How To Be Born Again*. Each Scripture-laced page ministered to my hurting heart as I began to understand that I was lost in sin and needed a Savior. As the truth of God's Word unfolded, the spiritual fog quickly evaporated. When God lifted the veil and opened my blind eyes, I finally understood the emptiness in my heart… I needed Jesus.

My thirsty soul absorbed the truth that Jesus loved me more than I could possibly comprehend. He gave His life for me – even before I acknowledged my need or desire for Him. All of my sin was thrust upon Jesus and nailed to the cross of Calvary.

The rugged cross I stared at as a child flooded my memory. I remembered asking, *Why did Jesus die? Who did this to Jesus?* My search for the truth ended as my heart filled with repentance. *My sin* put Jesus on the cross. He willingly took the punishment I deserved for my sin. I wept, realizing for the first time in my life that my Creator loved me. God did, in fact, exist.

Confessing the sinner's prayer out loud, I asked Jesus to come into my heart. Although I felt unworthy of His love, I knew He accepted the broken life I laid at His feet. Dropping to my knees, I surrendered my life to my Maker. As the light of the Word of God swallowed up my spiritual darkness, I met Jesus. The first chapter of my life in Christ had begun.

# CHAPTER 2
## Choose Jesus – Choose Life

**DO YOU *KNOW ABOUT* JESUS OR DO YOU *KNOW* JESUS?**
After dwelling in spiritual darkness for almost 20 years, I found life in Jesus Christ. Do you know Jesus Christ as your Lord and Savior? Have you taken the step from *knowing about* Him to *knowing* Him personally?

Eternally grateful for answers to the questions I pondered as a child and young adult, I finally understood why Jesus died on the rugged cross I had stared at in dismay. After years of searching for the truth, I not only knew about my Creator, but I discovered a truth even more wondrous: God wanted a personal relationship with me.

I want to share exciting news with you who may be searching for the truth.

### IN THE BEGINNING
In the beginning, God created man to enjoy a personal intimate relationship with Him. Adam and Eve walked with God; Adam and Eve talked with God. They were naked with no shame. The first man and woman shared close fellowship with their Creator.

God gave man dominion over the earth and blessed him with an abundant life. The Bible says, "God blessed them and said to them, 'Be fruitful and increase in number; fill the earth and subdue it. Rule over the fish of the sea and the birds of the air and over every living creature that moves on the ground'" (Genesis 1:28). Man had dominion in the earth… in the beginning.

### THE BAD NEWS – FALLEN MAN AND HIS SIN NATURE
Because Adam disobeyed God in the Garden of Eden, sin entered the earth. Through Adam's disobedience, dominion of the earth was

relinquished to Satan, who became the god of this world. 2 Corinthians 4:4 tells us Satan is the "god of this age." When man went his own willful way, his relationship with God was broken and his earthly dominion was stripped away. Adam's sin resulted in severe consequences for all of us.

Every human being is born with the sin nature that was passed down from Adam. We do not need to be taught to sin as it comes naturally to us. Young children are not trained to act selfishly, lie, hit, steal, and disobey, but instead are acting out of their sin nature.

Because God is a holy God, He cannot be in the presence of the sin that plagues us. Sin separates us from God. That's the bad news.

Many try to bypass the issue of sin through good works, religion, or morality. Were you taught that you could somehow work your way into heaven if you accumulated enough good deeds on your record sheet? Maybe you thought you could enter heaven's gates if you attended church on Sundays. Did someone explain that you could gain entrance to heaven only if you are good enough?

Regardless of how many good works you accomplish, how many church services you attend or how high your moral standards are, you are not righteous enough to be in God's presence. You cannot enter the kingdom of God through any of these methods as sin continues to separate you from God. *All* are sinners and *all* fall short of God's glory (Romans 3:23). You can search the world over and not find a man who has not sinned (Ecclesiastes 7:20). A sinless man does not exist, other than Jesus Christ of Nazareth.

Are you convinced you are heaven bound because you believe in God? Scripture says that even the demons believe there is one God and they shudder at His name (James 2:19). Satan surely knows there is one true God, yet his future is in the lake of fire where he will be tormented day and night forever and ever (Revelation 20:10). No, believing in God is not sufficient to enter eternal glory with the Father either.

Sinful man faces eternal death, eternal separation from God, eternal damnation. On his own, man is hopeless in his sin, with no possible avenue to remove sin and restore his relationship with God. Because God is a just God and must judge sin, man's sin had to be accounted for.

## THE GOOD NEWS – JESUS MADE A WAY

Good News arrived on the scene two thousand years ago. Wonderful news! Out of His unfailing love, God sent Jesus to the rescue. His only begotten Son, born of a virgin and without sin, was the only acceptable sacrifice for man's sin. The Lamb of God, the perfect, spotless lamb, was sent to take away the sin of the world. Jesus, the only one not deserving punishment, willingly endured the punishment man deserved.

Jesus Christ, God's only precious Son, shed His blood, was crucified and died on the cross, removing man's sin and making the way for eternal life. Every sin you ever committed or will commit was put upon Jesus. While you were still in sin, before you even recognized you were a sinner, Christ died for you (Romans 5:8).

Praise God – He made a way for you! Jesus made the *only* way possible. His blood washed away your sin. The Apostle John writes, "For God so loved the world that he gave his one and only Son, that whoever believes in him shall not perish but have eternal life" (John 3:16). What love He demonstrated!

Jesus bridged the once great chasm between God and man. His death brought us to God, where we can once again enjoy a personal intimate relationship with Him. 1 Peter 3:18 says, "For Christ died for sins once for all, the righteous for the unrighteous, to bring you to God." Because of Jesus' sacrifice, man's relationship with Father God was restored.

We can stand righteous before God only because of Jesus (2 Corinthians 5:21). Regardless of what attempts we make in our own strength, we could never do enough to deserve or earn God's forgiveness.

Glory to God – Jesus did not stay in the grave! He rose from the dead in victory over sin! Jesus died for our sins and was raised to life for our justification (Romans 4:25). The tomb is empty! Because Jesus lives, we can live.

## RECEIVING THE GIFT OF ETERNAL LIFE

God, the Creator of the universe, offered His Son as a sacrifice for sin because He loves you and desires a personal relationship with you. Although you deserve death and eternal separation from God,

He offers you life – the *gift* of eternal life through Christ Jesus (Romans 6:23). Eternal life in Christ is a gift.

If my neighbor, Ed, were dying of starvation, I wouldn't hesitate to buy food for him. As a demonstration of love, I would willingly sacrifice my finances to purchase the groceries he needed. Although I purchase food so Ed can live, it will do him no good until he receives my gift. In order to enjoy the full benefits, he must accept my gift, open it, and finally he must eat the food. Ed, of course, has the option of rejecting my gift, as I cannot force my gift of love. If he accepts my gift, he will live. If he rejects my gift, he will die.

In a similar way, you are dying in your sin. Without forgiveness of sin, you face eternal punishment and separation from God. God provided eternal life through the sacrifice of His only Son Jesus, but it's up to you to personally receive His gift. God will not force Himself into your life. He comes into man's heart to cleanse sin by invitation only. He offers you the gift of life. Will you receive it from Him? Will you make Jesus Lord of your life?

Have you opened the door of your heart to Jesus? He stands at the door knocking. If you open the door, He promises to come in (Revelation 3:20). If you have never repented of your sin and accepted Jesus as Savior, I invite you to make Jesus Lord of your life right now. If you want to accept God's gift of forgiveness and eternal life, pray this prayer out loud.

Father, I come to you in the Name of Jesus. I believe Jesus Christ is the Son of God. I know I'm a sinner and need your forgiveness. I'm sorry for my sin and want to turn from my sin. I believe Jesus died and was raised from the dead for my justification. I invite you to come into my heart right now to be Lord of my life. I believe with my heart and confess with my mouth Jesus as my Lord and Savior. Heavenly Father, fill me with your Holy Spirit. I receive everything you have for me. In Jesus Name. Amen!

## REJOICE IN THE ASSURANCE OF SALVATION

Now a part of the kingdom of God, you are a child of the King! You are born again and all heaven is rejoicing! (Luke 15:10). A party is going on in heaven right now!

You will never have to wonder if you will "make it" to heaven or not. Actually you could never make it on your own merit. None of us could earn our way into heaven because we *all* fall short of His glory. Paul tells us we are saved by the grace of God, not by works or good deeds. Salvation by grace is a gift from God (Ephesians 2:8).

Forgiveness and eternal life come only through Jesus. He is the *one and only* way. No one can see the Father except through Jesus (John 14:6). No person will ever see the kingdom of God unless he is born again (John 3:3). The *only* way to eternal glory is through Jesus. You must come into the kingdom through the cross of Calvary. Alternate routes to heaven are non-existent.

Are you wondering why you don't feel any different? Feelings are irrelevant because the new birth is not based on emotions. Being born again is an act of faith based on the truth of God's Word. Romans 10:9-10 says, "That if you confess with your mouth, 'Jesus is Lord,' and believe in your heart that God raised him from the dead, you will be saved. For it is with your heart that you believe and are justified, and it is with your mouth that you confess and are saved." By believing in and receiving Jesus, you gained the right to *become* God's child (John 1:12-13). According to the truth of God's Word, you are now a child of God!

Because you chose to accept the sacrifice Jesus made for you, you received the gift of eternal life. Clean before God as if you never sinned, God removed your transgression from you as far as the east is from the west (Psalm 103:12). Your sin is gone! Now in Christ, the old you is gone and the new you has come (2 Corinthians 5:17). You're a brand new creation!

## MORE BENEFITS!

Jesus took our destined eternal separation from God and gave us eternal life. If Jesus never did another thing for us, we would still have reason to shout for joy. Being forgiven and having eternal life with God to look forward to is enough for abundant joy. But there's more!

Isaiah's prophecy bursts with the blessings we received at the cross of Calvary: "Surely he hath borne our griefs, and carried our sorrows: yet we did esteem him stricken, smitten of God, and afflicted. But he was wounded for our transgressions, he was bruised for our iniquities: the chastisement of our peace was upon him; and with his stripes we are healed." (Isaiah 53:4-5, KJV).

Let's take a closer look at God's provision through the cross according to Isaiah's prophecy. If you have access to a study Bible that includes Hebrew and Greek translations, take it out and dust it off so you can fully discover the meaning behind this powerful scripture.

We already addressed the truth that Jesus took your sin upon Himself at the cross, but we must not overlook the other benefits He brings to you.

According to Isaiah's prophecy, Jesus "bore our griefs." The Hebrew word for bore is "nasa," which means to lift, carry away; cast away; ease; erase, or take away. The Hebrew word for griefs is "choliy," meaning sickness and diseases – any and all sickness in your body. Jesus bore ALL illness, affliction, wound, and injury at the cross. Since He took sickness and disease upon Himself, you do not need to tolerate these maladies in your body. Satan will surely try to inflict you with sickness and disease, but as you stand in faith and claim your rights and privileges as a born again believer you can enjoy perfect health.

Jesus also "carried our sorrows." The Hebrew word for sorrows is "makob" and means pain, suffering, sorrows, grief, pains, and woes. Jesus took all of that anguish upon Himself so you could be set free from them.

"The chastisement of our peace was upon Him." The suffering of Jesus at the cross brings you peace. The Hebrew translation of the word peace, "shalom," not only means peace as you may assume it to mean, but safety, prosperity, well-being, intactness, and wholeness as well. These blessings are yours because of the sacrifice Jesus made for you. You are protected, prosperous, and completely whole in Christ, Jehovah Shalom.

Praise God, "we are healed" by the stripes Jesus bore on his back! The Hebrew translation of healed (rapha) means to mend, cure, heal, repair and make whole. It is not the will of God for you to be sick. Jehovah Rapha made a way for you to walk in perfect health.

20

1 Peter 2:24 says you *were* healed by the stripes Jesus bore. *By His stripes, you were healed.* Jesus came, was crucified, and rose again, making healing past tense – YOU WERE HEALED! It is done! Don't continue to beg God to heal you as Jesus already did everything He's going to do about your healing. It's up to you to appropriate this tremendous blessing. God's provisions belong to you *now.* Grab hold of them!

The tremendous truth of healing through Jesus is repeated over and over again throughout scripture. Matthew 8:16-17 says, "He drove out the spirits with a word and healed all the sick. This was to fulfil what was spoken through the prophet Isaiah: 'He took up our infirmities and carried our diseases.'" As Jesus healed all who were sick, He fulfilled what Isaiah had spoken, Halleluia!

King David reminds us not to forget all of the benefits Jesus provided. He forgives ALL of your sins and heals ALL of your diseases. *ALL* (Psalm 103:2-3). Have you received the full benefits? Remember my neighbor Ed? In order for him to enjoy the full benefit of my gift, he had to receive it, open the package and appropriate what was inside. You too need to open the gift of Jesus to discover the full benefits He brings to you.

To further understand God's provision for health, we can look to the law He gave to Moses. God's law promised tremendous blessing to those who obeyed. I suggest you read them in Deuteronomy 28. The blessings are endless! Severe consequences awaited those who disobeyed however. Disease and sickness were among the grave consequences of disobedience.

Moses shares the consequences of disobedience in Deuteronomy 28:15-61: "If you do not obey the Lord your God and do not carefully follow all his commands and decrees I am giving you today, all these curses will come upon you and overtake you... The Lord will also bring on you every kind of sickness and disaster not recorded in this Book of the Law, until you are destroyed."

Sickness is a curse of the law. *Every* kind of sickness and disease is a curse of the law and a work of the enemy. Praise God, redemption from the curse of the law is part of our inheritance as believers in Jesus Christ! (Galatians 3:13-14). We are redeemed from the curse and set free!

These blessings are reason to shout for joy! Did you know your Savior provided so much for you? These abundant blessings belong to you through the blood of Jesus. They are yours right now. Have you received the gifts God provided in His precious Son Jesus?

## SALVATION IS MORE THAN FORGIVENESS OF SIN

Most born again Christians understand that salvation through Jesus brings forgiveness of sin and eternal life. Praise God forevermore! But many have not received their full inheritance that Jesus paid a great price for. Many are living in spiritual poverty, not realizing they were given a rich inheritance.

Romans 1:16 says, "I am not ashamed of the gospel, because it is the power of God for the salvation of everyone who believes: first for the Jew, then for the Gentile." If you study the Hebrew and Greek words for *salvation*, you will see the implication of the idea of deliverance, safety, preservation, healing, and soundness.

Consider a great truth as we look at Romans 1:16 again with this in mind: "I am not ashamed of the gospel, because it is the power of God for the salvation (and the power of God for the *deliverance,* and the power of God for the *safety,* and the power of God for the *preservation,* and the power of God for the *healing,* and the power of God for the *soundness)* of everyone who believes: first for the Jew, then for the Gentile." Halleluia, all of these tremendous blessings are available to *everyone who believes*. Do you believe? Salvation through Christ Jesus is abundant life in Him.

Can you believe and receive what Christ provided for you? It cost Jesus His life to give you these abundant blessings. In the coming chapters you will further discover how to appropriate the gifts God provided for you.

## FAITH IN THE TRUTH OR FAITH IN TRADITION

I spent many joyless years putting my faith in man's traditions and beliefs but found no victory or hope in man's methods. Man's ways change. Churches change and man's doctrines change. God's Word, the living Word that brings hope and victory in Christ Jesus, *never* changes. God Himself will never change (Malachi 3:6). Jesus Christ is the same today as He was yesterday. He is the same today as He will be forever (Hebrews 13:8).

The truth of God's Word is solid foundation for your entire life. It is unshakeable and immovable. His Word is eternal; it stands firm in the heavens (Psalm 119:89) and stands forever (1 Peter 1:25). When all else passes away, God's Word will still stand.

The following chapters will examine a number of aspects of the Christian journey into the Promised Land of victory. As you enter and possess the promises along the way, God's Word will light your path in search for the truth.

Rely on the Holy Spirit to help you understand the Scriptures. Jesus said, "The Counselor, the Holy Spirit, whom the Father will send in my name, will teach you all things and will remind you of everything I have said to you" (John 14:26). His Spirit will guide you into all truth (John 16:13).

I challenge you to examine your belief system as you read the following pages. Ask God to open the eyes of your heart as you determine why you believe what you believe. Are your beliefs based on man's word or on God's Word?

# CHAPTER 3
# I'm Saved... Now What?

People receive Jesus as Lord and Savior in diverse surroundings and varying circumstances. Some make Jesus Lord of their life during a church service altar call, some as individuals share the gospel, and others respond to an evangelist's message of salvation. Some people are born again when they are alone with God.

While some new birth experiences include a dramatic outward manifestation of God's presence, other experiences are a calm, serene encounter with God. The circumstances and surroundings really are not important, yet what follows the decision to follow Jesus is critical.

When I received Jesus into my heart, I was alone with God. At the time, I didn't attend church regularly, my circle of friends were not Christians, nor did I have any other form of discipleship to point me in the right direction. Although aware that a change had taken place in my heart, I was ignorant of what my next step should be. Lacking knowledge of the truth that God predestined me to be conformed to the likeness of His Son Jesus (Romans 8:29), my destiny in Christ remained hidden.

Immediately following my decision to accept Jesus as Lord, worldly distractions enticed me away from God. The evil one lurked in the background, determined to eradicate God's plan by steering me away from Jesus. Although the seed of God's Word was planted in my heart, Satan diligently sought to destroy the seed before it became fruitful.

In the parable of the sower (Matthew 13:19-23) Jesus likens His Word to a seed being sown by a farmer and highlights the different results that can follow. He explains what the parable of the sower means:

When anyone hears the message about the kingdom and does not understand it, the evil one comes and snatches away what was sown in his heart. This is the seed sown along the path. The one who received the seed that fell on rocky places is the man who hears the word and at once receives it with joy. But since he has no root, he lasts only a short time. When trouble or persecution comes because of the word, he quickly falls away. The one who received the seed that fell among thorns is the man who hears the word, but the worries of this life and the deceitfulness of wealth choke it, making it unfruitful. But the one who received the seed that fell on good soil is the man who hears the word and understands it. He produces a crop, yielding a hundred, sixty or thirty times what was sown.

Because the seed of God's Word had not taken root in my heart, I quickly fell away from the Lord. Painfully aware that sin remained in my life, I questioned whether I really was "born again," reasoning that if the new birth had taken place, I would no longer sin.

Satan convinced me that I had failed to measure up to God's expectations. Weighed down with guilt and condemnation, I assumed I was destined for hell once again. The cares of the world quickly swept me away from seeking the direction I needed in following Christ. Not attending church or involved in Christian fellowship, I began a span of several years of wandering in spiritual wilderness – but nobody noticed.

Continuing the same lifestyle I followed prior to receiving Jesus as Lord, I entered into a stormy, godless marriage. Fear, deception, and abuse quickly became part of my daily experience. Although allowed to attend church alone, I was often too weak to make the effort. When I did enter church doors to feed my spiritual starvation, I left unfed, unfilled and unsatisfied. The familiar repetitious prayers and traditions made church empty and lifeless for me.

Certain that God was angry with me for failing Him, I strayed further into the scorched desert of spiritual wilderness. Overcome with guilt, I knew I was following the wrong path but didn't know how to find the right path.

Returning to my place of comfort with the "in" crowd, I

participated in worldly activities in order to avoid the risk of being considered "different" or "religious." My peers and co-workers didn't realize that the pillar of strength they saw on the outside was slowly dying on the inside.

My decision to follow Jesus quickly became a faint memory. If poor choices cornered me in a crisis situation, however, I cried out to God, offering bargains in exchange for His rescue. My time of selfishly seeking God was self-centered and temporary though. I never followed through with my end of the bargain.

In the midst of a chaotic lifestyle, I gave birth to my firstborn son. The joy of his birth quickly turned to consternation and fear six weeks later when his father announced his immediate plans to move out of the house and out of my life. On my knees, I pleaded, desperately begging him not to leave our new son and me, but he left despite my efforts. The abrupt death of the marriage left only ashes of emotional pain and scars behind.

Alone and frightened, hopelessness saturated my heart. Outwardly though, the independent, confident person I projected continued to deceive those around me. Wiping my tears away and pushing fresh wounds of rejection aside, I poured myself once again into my career.

While I was consumed with inner grief and devastation, God faithfully continued working in the background of my tarnished life. Focussed on building a new life for my son and me, I thought God had forgotten about me. Unaware that God still held me in the palm of His mighty hand, I didn't see Him picking up the broken pieces of my life to rearrange them into a beautiful new life in Christ. God lovingly reached into my emotional storm and turned me to a season of renewal. Once again I found myself alone with God. He had my full attention.

## GOD ACCEPTS EVERYONE – DO YOU?

Many who come to Christ or return to Him after years of backsliding are broken as I was when my marriage ended. Multitudes have tried living their own independent way and, after great pain and suffering, finally surrender to God. Some who respond to God's call come into the body of Christ appearing unattractive or spiritually immature and unsettled. Do Christians judge them and sneer in disgust or take their hand and help them find a new life in Christ?

As God brings the end time harvest, many will enter church doors looking and acting much different than we may prefer. Prostitutes, drug addicts and dealers, child molesters and more will enter, searching for the hope and deliverance only Jesus can bring. God loves every one of them and sent His Son to give them life. Can you love them as well?

Jesus didn't hang out with the beautiful people. He surrounded Himself with the sinners and the unattractive: the prostitutes, the lepers, cheaters, and those suffering from mental and physical disease just to name a few. Jesus loved and accepted the people others rejected. Do you love and accept these people as Jesus did?

Do personal preferences hinder your willingness to demonstrate God's love and Christian discipleship? God rescued me from the pit of hell and transformed my life completely. He will transform *any* life. I was broken and discouraged when I re-entered church doors. Many broken and discouraged people will enter your church as well. How will you receive the people God brings into the body of Christ?

## PRODIGAL DAUGHTER RETURNS
## HOME TO FAITHFUL FATHER

While I healed from a broken marriage, God sent a remarkable man into my life that patiently helped me learn to love and to trust again. A divine gift from God, Tom's uncompromising integrity and tenderness of heart refreshed my soul. I admired his strength, compassion and unconditional love for those around him. God had a plan for us.

Early in our relationship, Tom's secretary invited us to a church service. At the end of the service, the pastor invited unbelievers to accept Jesus as Savior. Tom tearfully leaned over and whispered, "I want to go to the altar to accept Jesus. Come with me."

"I already accepted Jesus a long time ago." I hesitated, remembering the day I met Jesus at the cross. Nonetheless, we stepped into the aisle and made our way to the altar.

As we walked to the front of the church and confessed the sinner's prayer, God brought back to my remembrance the decision

I made to follow Christ several years before. My heart flooding with God's unfailing love, I remembered the cross. I remembered Jesus and the blood He shed for me.

Returning to my first love that glorious day, I recommitted my life to Christ. As my husband-to-be accepted Jesus as Lord of his life, I came back to Jesus. I, the prodigal daughter, ran into the open arms of my heavenly Father who patiently and lovingly waited for my return. Vowing to never leave Him again, I purposed in my heart to know the One who gave His life for me. For the first time, I opened a Bible.

Throughout the years of wandering in spiritual wilderness, I neglected my Savior, yet He never left me or forgot about me. Looking back, I saw God's comforting touch throughout every thread of pain I endured, realizing His divine hand of protection saved me from many life-threatening situations. God was faithful even when I was not faithful. He never stopped loving me and never gave up on me. Are you a prodigal child? God loves you and believes in you! He wants you to come home.

## DISCIPLESHIP MAKES A DIFFERENCE

Tom and I entered into Christian marriage with pure joy. God glued us together and became the very core of our covenant relationship. Determined that every aspect of our lives would revolve around God and His Word, we were confident that regardless of what we might face, God would see us through.

Joining a Bible-believing church, we were discipled by other believers who were further along on the Christian journey. We saturated ourselves in the Scriptures, as our hunger to know Jesus grew deeper.

Attending Bible studies and enjoying fellowship with other believers helped us gain knowledge of God's Word and to submit to God's Word. As our minds were renewed by the Word of God and applied to our daily life, a tremendous transformation took place. Lying aside our worldly ways, we chose God's ways. Many choices were not easy to make; we often wrestled with overcoming our flesh as we learned to obey.

We quickly discovered that a life committed to Christ was not void of trials. When trials and tests stretched us, our brothers and sisters in Christ encouraged and supported us with unconditional love, helping us realize we were not on the journey alone. Through dedicated discipleship and God's grace, we grew in Christian maturity.

Discipleship lacked in my life as a new Christian and resulted in having to endure many tough places alone. What a difference it could have made earlier in my life if even one believer had recognized my need for a spiritual mentor and made the sacrifice to help me get started in the right direction.

Because of the absence of discipleship I stumbled on the wrong path for several years *after* accepting Jesus as Savior. The earth is filled with undiscipled Christians who, although they are born again and heaven bound, never grow in Christian maturity. Multitudes of spiritually hungry people accept Christ at the altar, yet exit the doors of the church never to be seen again. Many never complete their course, partly because the Church fails to realize the importance of discipleship.

Christians rejoice when a person publicly confesses Jesus as Lord, yet they sometimes forget that the devil is waiting outside the door to steal what that new babe in Christ received. The devil prowls around, waiting for an opportunity to steer new Christians on the wrong path where he can steal, kill and destroy. It's Satan's mission.

The Bible warns, "Be sober, be vigilant; because your adversary the devil walks about like a roaring lion, seeking whom he may devour" (1 Peter 5:8, NKJV). Be on the lookout for the wolf trying to attack baby sheep coming into the fold!

Many new believers are left at the altar. Doesn't anybody care? Is the rest of the flock too busy with their own lives to help the new babes find the right path? How many new Christians are wandering in spiritual wilderness or suffering in a life of sin because they lack discipleship? Multitudes!

Mature Christians must surround new believers immediately after they make a commitment to serve Jesus. We cannot leave them at the altar! New Christians need to be encouraged and taught by spiritually mature role models. They are just beginning the journey of transforming their lives into the image of Jesus Christ.

Christians must make time to take a new believer by the hand and lead him into the truth of the God's Word. The Master instructed us to make disciples of all nations and to teach those disciples everything He commanded (Matthew 28:18-20). The body of Christ must get this command engrained in their heart! Jesus told us to make disciples of all nations. Getting people born again is only the first step.

## A BABY BORN IN THE FLESH

When a baby is born, he is nurtured, taught, and showered with much tender care and attention. A baby is not punished for wetting his diaper or for making mistakes during his learning process, but instead is taught, trained and encouraged into desired behaviors.

Is a baby condemned because he falls down and scrapes his knee? Certainly not! He is helped up and given gentle love and attention to recover and continue his journey. The long-term goal for a baby is to mature into an adult through a process that includes multiple stages of growth. Several years pass before a child enters kindergarten and many more come and go before he is prepared to enter college.

## A BABY BORN IN THE SPIRIT

When a person is born again, he is born a spiritual baby. As he feeds on God's Word, prays and testifies about what God has done for him, he grows spiritually. He needs to be nurtured, taught, and given much tender care and attention just as a natural baby does. A newborn believer must grow and mature spiritually just as he grows and matures in the natural. He will likely fall down and stumble many times during the various stages of spiritual growth. He, too, needs to be helped up and loved during his process of growth.

The teaching, training, and encouragement a new believer receives from his brothers and sisters in Christ are critical to his spiritual growth. A new believer benefits greatly from the experience and encouragement of more mature believers. Seasoned believers can play a key role in the new believer's spiritual maturing process. Their encouragement may determine whether a struggling believer continues his journey in Christ or quits in hopelessness.

## ENCOURAGEMENT MAKES A DIFFERENCE

When my son Joseph was five years old, he participated in his first swimming lessons. Throughout the lessons, his hunger for and need of encouragement quickly became apparent.

Since it was Joe's first exposure to swimming, he hesitated to even dip his face in the water. Each time the patient swimming instructor told Joseph to perform a new skill in the water, he nervously completed the task to the best of his ability and then looked to see if I was watching.

I never failed to cheer him on or to give him the thumbs up sign when he looked back for my approval. If he failed at a task, I exhorted him to try again. My encouragement prodded Joseph to excellence.

In a similar way, new believers take comfort in knowing his brothers and sisters in the Lord are willing to take his hand and lead him into a new life in Christ. For some, life in Christ is a drastic change and through the beginning phases of transformation, encouragement from other believers is critical.

It is wise for a new believer to find a mature Christian to mentor him through this time of growth. The security and comfort of knowing his spiritual family will restore him instead of rejecting him when he makes a mistake is more critical than many realize.

## FOLLOW GODLY ROLE MODELS

Role models impact your journey in Christ Jesus. If you want to reflect Jesus, seek role models that look like Jesus. Does your role model offer godly counsel? Does he practice the qualities you need to develop? Is he a doer of the Word of God? Does she reflect the image of Jesus? Spend time with her, watch her, and talk to her about the things you wrestle with. How did she find victory in these areas? You can avoid much error by learning from mature Christians with proven victory in areas you are weak in.

If you need marriage counsel, find a couple who exemplifies a strong marriage, not a couple whose marriage is in the torrential rain of disaster. If you're facing financial difficulties, find a mentor or two with financial wisdom and demonstrated financial balance, not someone with a mountain of overdue bills who continues charging up his credit cards.

If you need to get your house in order, get help from people whose house is in order, not from people whose house is dysfunctional and calamitous. One cannot lead another to a place he hasn't arrived at himself. Beware! Many pamper their misery by surrounding themselves with others' misery. Misery loves company.

Is a mature Christian mentor better than a new Christian? No! Smarter? No! More spiritual? Certainly not! He's simply further along on the journey in Christ and able to help a newer believer learn from his experience by pointing him to Jesus.

Seeking role models that sharpen and challenge you in the things of God provokes spiritual maturity. Godly wisdom and experience are invaluable so don't allow pride to stop you from seeking spiritual guidance.

You may face trials that require you to ask your brothers and sisters in Christ for help. Are you willing to turn to your brothers and sisters when faced with trial? Pride can provoke you to fight your battles alone, but remember: The body of Christ is a family. We must support our family members and allow them to support us.

Tom was once building a deck and patio when he faced a mountain of a challenge. A 4'X4' slab of dense concrete sat where the new patio was to be poured. Unable to proceed with his project until the 5" thick slab was moved, Tom attempted to move the weighty mountain using his own methods. Utilizing a sledgehammer, he tried to break it into smaller, easier to move pieces, but could not even put a dent into the massive mountain. On his own, the task was impossible. Alone, all attempts failed.

A Christian brother heard of Tom's challenge and arrived at our home with four willing and strong men. Joining their strength together, they moved the stubborn slab to its new location in less than five minutes. Working together, they moved the mountain with ease. An impossible task for Tom alone was of minimal effort when he allowed his brothers to help.

Using their God-given strength, the men worked together and got the job done. God ultimately gets the job done, but His children's willingness to work together in supporting and helping each other is key.

You are God's hands and feet. Are you willing to help others and willing to allow others to help you? You need your brothers and sisters in Christ and your brothers and sisters in Christ need you, as you are all part of the same body.

## SEEK A MENTOR AND BE A MENTOR

Discipleship promotes accountability in the body of Christ. As we hold one another accountable to God's plan and exhort each other to excellence, the chance of stumbling off the path of righteousness is minimized. Loving accountability through discipleship encourages us to keep God's Word active and sharp. King Solomon spoke a great truth regarding discipleship: "As iron sharpens iron, so one man sharpens another" (Proverbs 27:17). A good mentor is one who loves you enough to hold you accountable to the plan of God.

Regardless of how long you've been a Christian, consider involvement in some type of discipleship program and be open to discipling and mentoring others. You may say, "But I'm a new believer myself! God can't use me." Even if you were born again yesterday, God can use you powerfully to magnify the Name of Jesus. You have a testimony to share! You don't need to be a Bible scholar to be used of God. He'll use you right where you are!

# CHAPTER 4
## Out With The Old – In With The New

As a new believer, I knew I had missed it somewhere. *If I'm really saved and Jesus is in my heart, then why am I still sinning?* I thought. *Christians are supposed to be perfect, aren't they?*

How frustrating and confusing to realize I was capable of sinning after being born again. I was *supposed* to be a new creation. The old me was *supposed* to be gone and the new me was *supposed* to have come. In fact, most of the new me was still the old me after giving my life to the Lord. I was a mess before I was born again and a mess after being born again. God had much work to do in me.

### THE DEVIL'S TRAP OF DECEPTION

The devil slyly sets traps of deceptive condemnation for new believers. The evil one strives to convince the newborn believer that he is the same old sinful person he was before accepting Christ. Provoking hopeless condemnation, Satan attempts to block Christians from the knowledge or understanding of their new identity in Christ Jesus.

Has the devil tried to convince you that you aren't saved? Satan whispers, "So sorry, but your heart just isn't pure enough for God. Look at yourself, you unworthy lost soul, you're still sinning! If you really meant that confession of faith, you wouldn't be sinning anymore. You're just not good enough!"

Has the accuser brought past sin to your remembrance, trying to convince you that it's simply too big to be covered by the blood of Jesus? "Hah, you sinner!" Satan sneers, "Don't you remember that lie you told? Remember the time you cheated? Remember the sin… you know the one I'm talking about… that one isn't covered by the blood! It goes beyond God's limits… so sorry." Satan is a thief who comes only to steal and kill and destroy (John 10:10). He wants to steal from you.

The devil is the father of lies. Has he lied to you? Satan hungers to strip God's blessings from you – but he can't! He cannot rob you of the abundant life God purchased for you at the cross. It's impossible for Satan to snatch you away from the omnipotent God who saved you and holds you close in the palm of His mighty hand.

Jesus assures our safety in Him: "My sheep listen to my voice; I know them, and they follow me. I give them eternal life, and they shall never perish; no one can snatch them out of my hand" (John 10:27-28). You belong to God and are safe in His protective hand.

## ENTRANCE INTO A LIFE-LONG
## JOURNEY IN CHRIST

Although the devil cannot snatch anyone out of God's hand, he focuses on deceiving and stealing from new believers in any way he can. He attempts to thwart God's plan and purpose by hindering Christian's spiritual growth.

A newborn believer must surround himself with more mature believers who will help him get firmly established in his Christian walk. He must gain understanding of his identity in Christ and realize that he has only begun a life-long journey. Without this revelation, discouragement and self-condemnation is common.

If a little lamb wanders away from the rest of the sheep, the wolf has easy access to devour him. Likewise, if a new babe in Christ wanders off into isolation while the rest of the flock pays no attention, he becomes a prime target for the devil.

Let's squelch the devil's lie. The cigarette you may still be smoking or the wine you continue to sip on will not keep you out of the kingdom of God. The only way of missing eternal life with our heavenly Father is by rejecting His Son Jesus. The destructive habits you still practice can, and will, be overcome through Jesus Christ. He will catapult you to victory.

Most Christians could use a major spiritual makeover after coming to the Lord. Be comforted in knowing God loves you and will help you conform to His image. He knows you better than you know yourself and understands the struggles and temptations you experience. As a man, Jesus was tempted *in every way* you are tempted (Hebrews 4:15). Jesus understands what you face. He's been there already.

God is not in heaven cracking the whip and shaking His fist because you haven't straightened out your life quickly enough. He will love and guide you through every step of your Christian journey. God patiently walks with you day by day, even when you stumble.

God sees you as the person you are yet to become in Him. He created you to be conformed to the likeness of Jesus (Romans 8:29). Halleluia, you are predestined to be like Him! Conforming to the likeness of Jesus is not an overnight miracle though. It's a day-by-day process of growth.

## HOW DO BELIEVERS DEAL WITH SIN?

Born again Christians do sin. How glorious it would be if you were instantly perfected! But it's simply not a reality. Although you sin, it doesn't mean you aren't saved or that you are a worthless failure. It indicates you are an imperfect human.

Confession of sin is not a one-time event that happens only at the new birth. When you sin, you must cleanse yourself through confession in order to maintain communion with God. Take your sin back to the cross of Calvary where Jesus shed His blood for your forgiveness. His blood washes the stain of sin and makes it white as snow. When you call your sin by name and repent, God will forgive you (1 John 1:9) and enable you to approach His holy presence freely again.

How unpleasant it would be if one went long periods of time without bathing! After a couple of weeks, few could tolerate being near him because of the stench. It's unpleasant when we fail to cleanse ourselves spiritually as well. Unconfessed sin creates a stench in our lives. Cleansing of sin should be part of every believer's daily spiritual hygiene. God is faithful. Meet Him at the cross.

Unconfessed sin can result in stifled prayer, failure to attend church, lack of commitment in serving God, and avoidance of Christian fellowship. Sin hinders fellowship with God and with those around us. It also creates an opportunity for Satan, the accuser of the brethren, to amplify condemnation. Cleansing of sin through the blood of Jesus frees you from the consequences of unconfessed sin.

Don't be afraid to approach God after you sin. God's throne of grace is exactly where you need to go! If sin is blocking the path between you and God, confess it and then run into your Father's open arms. The blood Jesus shed enables you to come boldly before God's throne. Don't be weighed down with guilt. Instead, confess your sin and be clean again (Proverbs 28:13). If you confess sin, you always find mercy. Go to Him, any time and any place. His mercies are new every morning, praise God!

## WHY DO CHRISTIANS SIN?

In order to understand why we sin after the new birth, we need to consider three components of salvation.

*The Spirit:* First, man is a spirit being. The spirit man is the inner man, our heart – our communion with God. Our spirit is born of imperishable seed the moment we are born again through the living and enduring word of God (1 Peter 1:23).

Birth in the Spirit is not the same as birth in the flesh for flesh gives birth to flesh, but the Spirit gives birth to spirit (John 3:6). When we are born again, our spirit is recreated as God places His very nature in us. The Spirit of God is tabernacled in our spirit at the new birth. Paul reminds us that we are God's temple and that God's Spirit lives in us (1 Corinthians 3:16). The Spirit of God dwells within you!

*The Body:* Secondly, we live in a physical body. Obviously our physical body did not change when we were born again. We look the same after we are born again as we looked before we were born again. Although inwardly we are being renewed day by day, our bodies are gradually deteriorating and wasting away (2 Corinthians 4:16). What's going on outside is much different than what's going on inside.

Our bodies will be glorified when we are raised up at the resurrection as Paul tells us in 1 Corinthians 15:42-44: "So will it be with the resurrection of the dead. The body that is sown is perishable, it is raised imperishable; it is sown in dishonor, it is raised in glory; it is sown in weakness, it is raised in power; it is sown a natural body, it is raised a spiritual body." Our lowly bodies will be transformed to the likeness of the glorious body of Jesus (Philippians 3:20-21). The glorification of our bodies is coming, praise God!

*The Soul:* The area bringing most confusion in understanding the new birth is the third area, the salvation of our soul. The soul consists of our mind, will and emotions and is separate from our spirit (Hebrews 4:12). Although many talk about the soul and spirit as being the same, they are not the same as we see again in 1 Thessalonians 5:23. "May your whole spirit, soul and body be kept blameless at the coming of our Lord Jesus Christ."

Sanctification takes place as you set yourself apart for God and choose to do what God wants you to do instead of what you want to do. You do not become super spiritual and develop super faith overnight. Salvation of your soul is a progressive work and must be worked out day by day (Philippians 2:12). Sanctification of your soul is a life-long and on-going process.

Renewing your mind by meditating on and confessing Scripture is a key to successfully working out your salvation. As God's Word renews your mind and is applied to your life, the characteristics of your old self gradually fall away. You may be surprised when the desire to participate in destructive activities no longer exists.

A wondrous miracle happens as you renew your mind: God's desires become your desires! When God's nature is birthed inside of you, it changes you. But remember: It takes time. *A lifetime.*

## SPIRITUAL GROWTH IS AN ON-GOING PROCESS

You continually learn, grow, and mature throughout the Christian journey. After conquering one area of growth, don't get too comfortable and think your growing time is complete. It won't be long before the Lord gently reveals another area needing change.

Until you take your last breath, God continues to teach you new revelations so you can complete your course. If you fail to mature in one area God reveals to you, He will bring more situations into your life that present the opportunity to bring you to the spiritual maturity He desires for you. God will test and retest you. If you fail the test, don't fret! You'll be given the opportunity to retest. God believes in you and *never* gives up on you!

You are God's precious child. He cares about you and will help you find victory in every area of your life. Be patient with yourself! Normally the bad habits you practiced before you were born again don't automatically disappear after the new birth, but hope for change is abundant through Christ.

We once had an unattractive crabapple tree in our front yard. We considered cutting it down because although it flowered for a short time in the spring, it was an eyesore the remainder of the year. Its wiry branches reached in every direction. Several thick branches shot out from the main trunk, making it even more unappealing. It held no shape whatsoever and was simply ugly.

I decided to make an attempt at giving my homely tree a makeover. With shears in hand, I began a process of pruning my ugly tree, sawing off the thick branches that tried to choke out the main trunk. I snipped here and snipped there, eliminating branches that didn't belong. Much to my surprise, my little eyesore endured a complete transformation and became a beautiful addition to our yard.

We, like my ugly little tree, need God's pruning. Some of our unpruned characteristics can be quite unattractive and hard for others to look at. Our spiritual fruit may be minimal or rotting on the branch. If we allow ugly areas of our lives to get overgrown by refusing God's pruning, our main lifeline will be choked out and our fruit will wither.

God prunes us so we can be transformed into the image of His precious Son Jesus. Jesus said, "I am the true vine, and my Father is the gardener. He cuts off every branch in me that bears no fruit, while every branch that does bear fruit he prunes so that it will be even more fruitful (John 15:1-2). God snips a bit here and a bit there and before you know it, you reflect Jesus through God's makeover.

When a fruit tree is pruned, its roots reach deeper, resulting in bigger and more plentiful fruit. Likewise, by submitting to God's pruning, our roots reach deeper into our foundation in Christ and results in a greater harvest of spiritual fruit. It is for God's glory that we bear much fruit as we show ourselves to be His disciples (John 15:8).

God's pruning can be a bit painful, as it was for my little tree. But if we allow God to chisel away the parts of us that don't look like Him, the end result is an incredible transformation into a beautiful reflection of Jesus.

## ALCOHOL ABUSE PUT TO DEATH

Alcohol abuse was an area of my life in desperate need of pruning. I was deceived in thinking I could embrace this destructive habit while living an abundant Christian life at the same time. Downing pitchers of margaritas while boasting of the transformation God made in me, my Christian words contradicted my carnal actions.

For a time I denied the fact that alcohol didn't belong in my life, yet I knew in my heart I was living a double life. Abusing alcohol and the consequences resulting from it were destroying my Christian witness and testimony. How effective was my testimony of the change Jesus made in my life when this destructive habit still followed me? Conviction stirred in my heart as God prepared me for change.

Not only was overindulging in alcohol not God's best for me, but it also provided a weapon for the devil to induce guilt and condemnation. After alcohol binges, I was plagued with severe guilt and self-condemnation. Consumed with shame, it became difficult facing God for forgiveness since I had promised to quit drinking countless times already. I realized that if I didn't lay this habit aside, the devil could use it as a tool to destroy me.

Realizing I faced a critical choice, I possessed no ability to turn from alcohol in my own strength. Conviction filled my heart when I remembered the many times I promised God I would cut alcohol out of my life. Most of my empty promises were made while in the midst of a guilt-saturated hangover.

Although I didn't know how to purge alcohol from my life, my growing hunger and thirst for Jesus strengthened me and propelled me to trust God for the impossible. What was impossible through my own efforts would be made possible through Him.

Humbly submitting myself to God, I surrendered the alcohol, vowing that it would never touch my lips again under any circumstance. Although I had made this promise to God many times in the past, it was different this time: I had counted the cost.

Without alcohol, part of my old life would die; my surroundings would change. Some friendships would become distant or be eliminated completely. I said good-bye to alcohol and was introduced to the person God created me to be in Him.

Laying alcohol down at the cross, I waved the white flag in surrender. Pushing alcohol aside once and for all, I looked up to the heavens with joy, knowing a critical choice had finally been settled. Entering a new season of my journey in Christ free from the bondage of alcohol, I would never be the same again.

## TAKE OFF THE OLD SELF AND PUT ON THE NEW SELF

As I chose God over alcohol, God's grace and mercy poured into my life. Completely delivered from the desire for alcohol, I pledged to live a sanctified life, set apart for God's use. With an earnest desire to fulfill my destiny in Christ, I felt born again all over again. I took off part of the old self and prepared to discover my new self.

Colossians 3:5-10 describes the process of taking off the old self and putting on the new self: "Put to death, therefore, whatever belongs to your earthly nature: sexual immorality, impurity, lust, evil desires and greed, which is idolatry. Because of these, the wrath of God is coming. You used to walk in these ways, in the life you once lived. But now you must rid yourselves of all such things as these: anger, rage, malice, slander, and filthy language from your lips. Do not lie to each other, since you have taken off your old self with its practices and have put on the new self, which is being renewed in knowledge in the image of its Creator."

The old shabby clothing from our old self must be taken off and laid down. Just as you wouldn't put on a beautiful new coat until you took off the old tattered one, you cannot put on your new self until the old self is taken off.

What does it mean to put on the new self? God tells us how to clothe ourselves in Colossians 3:12-14. "Therefore, as God's chosen people, holy and dearly loved, clothe yourselves with compassion, kindness, humility, gentleness and patience. Bear with each other and forgive whatever grievances you may have against one another. Forgive as the Lord forgave you. And over all these virtues put on love, which binds them all together in perfect unity." What a wardrobe of virtues to be clothed with!

As you renew your mind by the Word of God and apply it to your life, the process of taking off the old self and putting on the new self continues. Those parts of the old self not reflecting the image of Jesus must be put to death. The stubborn old self craves to be revived but you must choose to keep him and his fleshly desires dead. When those ungodly, fleshly desires rear their ugly heads, they must be crucified.

The Apostle Paul says, "You were taught, with regard to your former way of life, to put off your old self, which is being corrupted by its deceitful desires; to be made new in the attitude of your minds; and to put on the new self, created to be like God in true righteousness and holiness" (Ephesians 4:22-24). As you take off the old self and put on the new Christlike self, God's attributes will increasingly flow through your life. When people look at you, they will see Jesus!

Use godly wisdom and discernment as you develop the new self you were created to be in Christ. If you laid aside pornography and sexual immorality, have you rid your environment of those temptations or do you make excuses for keeping a few pornographic movies or magazines hidden in the closet? Is the Internet a hook in your mouth? What steps have you taken to ensure you will not fall into that trap? If drugs or alcohol were left at the cross, have you removed them from your home? Are you spending time at the local bar? What environments are you putting yourself in where temptations may entice you?

It wouldn't be wise for a dieting obese person to frequent a bakery where the aroma of fresh doughnuts lures him to indulge in delicacies that will harm him. Likewise, it's unwise to surround yourself with the obstacles you are trying to overcome. Have you encouraged revival of the old self by creating an atmosphere where he thrives? Use wisdom, as the flesh is strongwilled and rebellious.

## CONFLICT OF THE FLESH AND THE SPIRIT

Your flesh and the Spirit dwelling within you continually war with one another. Paul explains this truth in his letter to the Galatians: "So I say, live by the Spirit, and you will not gratify the desires of the sinful nature. For the sinful nature desires what is contrary to the Spirit, and the Spirit what is contrary to the sinful nature. They are in conflict with each other, so that you do not do what you want" (Galatians 5:16-17).

The flesh cries and screams like a spoiled brat because it wants you to pick up what you left at the cross. The flesh lusts after destructive vices. Just as a spoiled brat must be tempered and controlled, your flesh must be tempered and controlled. If the Spirit is not in control, the flesh will bully you around, stomp its feet and demand to get its way.

The sinful nature and fleshly desires do not disappear when you are born again. It is up to you, however, to determine whether the flesh or the Spirit will prevail. Who is in control of your life? Your flesh or the Spirit dwelling within you?

Alcohol had a strong hold on me as a new believer and could have crippled me if I had not put it to death. Are you embracing something that holds you back from the abundant life in Christ? Is there anything you have been unable to overcome or completely surrender? Are you nursing hidden sin? Maybe it's time to make some choices. Take it to the cross. God is there to help you. Victory awaits you at the cross of Calvary.

## CONDEMNATION VS CONVICTION

When you purpose to make godly choices, the enemy attempts to veer you off course by bringing temptation across your path, especially during weak moments. Jesus, hungry and weak after fasting forty days and forty nights in the desert, was tempted by the devil. What did the devil tempt him with? Food! How did Jesus resist temptation? He spoke the Word of God (Matthew 4:1-11).

God always sends help in times of temptation. You will never be tempted beyond what you can bear; God will always provide a way of escape (1 Corinthians 10:13). Jesus suffered when he was tempted, and is willing and able to help you when you are being tempted (Hebrews 2:18). Call on Him and He will answer.

As you choose to follow God's plan, the enemy diligently attempts to influence you through condemnation. Satan, the accuser, devours every opportunity to magnify your errors. If you sense condemnation in an area you wrestle with, know it is *not* God condemning you, as there is no condemnation for those who are in Christ Jesus (Romans 8:1).

Condemnation and conviction are vastly different. Conviction is from God, who loves you and wants the very best for you. Conviction brings an awareness of sin, which leads to repentance. Conviction, when responded to, results in victorious life in Christ.

Condemnation is from Satan, whose primary objective is to foil God's plan by defeating you. Condemnation induces shame, hopelessness, guilt, and unworthiness. Condemnation, if not resisted, leads to discouragement and ultimate defeat. Confusing conviction with condemnation enables the devil to shame believers into thinking they are unworthy.

The voice of the enemy speaks defeat; the voice of God speaks victory. Jesus, the greatest One, lives within you and walks with you through every temptation. God never condemns you for making a mistake but instead loves you with an everlasting and unfailing love.

## CHANGE REQUIRES ACTION ON YOUR PART

Conforming to the image of Jesus Christ requires change, and change requires action. As you renew your mind by God's Word, you must respond to God's Word by *acting* on God's Word. Knowing what the Bible says is not enough, you must practice it as well.

Do you need deliverance from alcohol as I did? Is deliverance from pornography what you desire? Have you fallen into an adulterous affair? Seeking God's help and joining with others in prayer will strengthen you to overcome strongholds, but you play a key role in your deliverance. You play a *significant* role. Only you can choose to change. God is not going to make your choices for you.

When you feel your conscience pricked, ask God to reveal what needs to change and how to change it. Repent by turning from your sin and then head in a new direction by implementing God's ways. If you fail, get back up and try again. God never says, "Ok, that's it! I've given you chance after chance and you're still failing me. You've repented of this before and here you are doing it again! I'm giving up on you!"

Your patient and loving Lord forgives and restores you regardless of your failures. God is your greatest fan and is always there to cheer you on. You can do all things through Christ who strengthens you (Philippians 4:13). You are an overcomer!

## GOD IS NOT MAD AT YOU!

Maybe you strayed onto the wrong path because you lacked discipleship as I did. Are you plagued with sin or suffering the consequences of poor choices? Don't condemn yourself! *God is not mad at you and hasn't given up on you!* His love for you is an everlasting love! Repent and turn back to God. Regardless of what you've done, as you come to Him with a repentant heart, God will not condemn you (Romans 8:1). *No condemnation*!

God lovingly welcomes you back with arms open wide. He is waiting for your return, just as He was waiting for me. He says, "Come." Run to Him. Don't let the devil steal one more day. Regardless of how you started as a new creature in Christ Jesus, God is faithful and will work even your biggest mistakes into good (Romans 8:28). The moment you turn back to Him with a repentant heart, He washes you clean once again.

The reasons you strayed really don't matter – just turn back to God. His plan and destiny for you have been established. Put the past in the past and start afresh right now. Forget the things from the past and reach forward to the things that are ahead (Philippians 3:13-14). Today is a new day!

## COUNT THE COST

Do you hunger to be like Jesus? What are you willing to sacrifice for God's purpose? How much effort are you willing to invest in your Christian journey? Count the cost. The price to completely surrendering your will to Jesus is high. What is the cost? *Everything*. You must be willing to give all and surrender all to enjoy the fullness of God. As you become increasingly dependent on the Lord Jesus, your spiritual growth becomes increasingly evident. The more you surrender to Him, the more you look like Him.

God called you to a sanctified life of holiness. As you take off the old self and put on the new self, surrender all to Him, friend in Christ, and see Him change you from glory to glory.

# CHAPTER 5
# His Word Settles It

## DO YOU BELIEVE THE BIBLE?

Faithful Christians believe the Holy Bible is true. Right? What about you? Do you take God at His Word from Genesis to Revelation? Are you convinced not only that God's Word is true, but that it is true in your life personally? You must decide if you wholeheartedly believe the Word of God is the absolute truth.

It is not unusual to discover Biblical truths that are difficult to grasp with the limited human mind. When facing Biblical challenges, do you automatically disregard the areas that stretch your faith or do you believe, by faith, that God's Word is true just because He is God?

Do you pick and choose which parts of the Bible you will believe? Do you disregard the portions of Scripture that your natural mind can't quite grasp? Christians often slice out the pages of the Bible that provoke their faith to grow. "Well..." some say, "Of course I believe the Bible... but... that prosperity stuff isn't true."

"Why, of course the Bible is true!" others claim, "but things like healing and miracles have passed away, it doesn't apply to us today."

Can you simply ignore the portions of God's Word that you find hard to believe? If unbelief causes you to slice out one portion here and another portion there, you'll be left holding only a few pages of truth. Can you enjoy God's abundant life and boldly stand against Satan with a few personally selected pages of truth? No! Aborting *any* of the Bible shortchanges you from God's best.

Are you expecting the natural from a supernatural God? Do you trust in the limited soulish realm of the natural or in the supernatural realm of the Creator? Basing faith on sight, feelings or mental reasoning will cause you to lose the fight of faith, as man's senses and reasoning often contradict God's Word.

Because God's ways are not man's ways, spiritual truth must be accepted by faith. God instructs Christians to walk by faith, not by sight (2 Corinthians 5:7). The righteous must live by faith (Romans 1:17).

People often accept anything and everything they are taught while growing up as the truth. Wisdom, however, will lead you to search Scripture to determine the real truth. God's Word is truth! (John 17:17).

## HEALING, PROSPERITY AND MIRACLES ARE FOR TODAY

Do you believe in forgiveness of sin but can't quite embrace the truth that your physical health was also provided through the cross? Maybe someone told you that God teaches lessons through sickness or punishes you through pain and suffering. Would you teach your own child a lesson by putting sickness on him? Would you punish him by striking him with a disease? What do you believe?

Were you taught that it's God's will for you to be sick? If it's God's will for you to endure sickness, does that mean you're trying to take yourself out of God's will if you visit the doctor or take medication? If you really believed sickness was God's will, you would have to remain sick to stay in His will, wouldn't you? What a silly thought!

If God willed sickness and disease, then Jesus defeated His own will as He healed those who were sick and oppressed of the devil (Acts 10:38). Jesus came to give life, and life more abundantly (John 10:10) – are you living the abundant life while sick and suffering in pain? Jesus instructed you to go into all the nations to preach the gospel. How can you go to the nations, or even your next-door neighbors, if you're sick and wracked with pain? What do you believe?

Do you struggle with the truth that God intends for you to prosper in every arena of your life? Maybe you were taught that you must be poor to be humble. There's no doubt that Abraham, Solomon and David would have a tough time believing God wanted them to be poor.

God blessed His faithful servants! God is no respecter of persons and will treat you no differently than he treated your forefathers. Jesus came to give *abundant* life. Living in poverty with your needs unmet and bill collectors pounding at your door is *not* abundant life. What do you believe?

Don't be deceived. God *never* causes you to endure something that Jesus already paid the price for at the cross. He will *never* make you sick, He will *never* bring you to poverty. He will *never* put anything on you that He redeemed you from at the cross. *Never*!

Have you bought into the idea that healing and miracles passed away when the last of the 12 disciples died? I challenge you to search the Bible from Genesis to Revelation for this doctrine. You will not find it. Try convincing someone that was miraculously healed by the hand of God that healing or miracles have passed away. They will likely chuckle. Why? They already know the truth!

God placed the gift of healings, miraculous powers, and other spiritual gifts in the body of Christ. "Now to each one the manifestation of the Spirit is given for the common good. To one there is given through the Spirit the message of wisdom, to another the message of knowledge by means of the same Spirit, to another faith by the same Spirit, to another gifts of healing by that one Spirit, to another miraculous powers, to another prophecy, to another distinguishing between spirits, to another speaking in different kinds of tongues, and to still another the interpretation of tongues. All these are the work of one and the same Spirit, and he gives them to each one, just as he determines" (1 Corinthians 12:7-11). God's miraculous gifts are bestowed on us for the common good... both then and now.

## SIGNS FOLLOW THOSE WHO BELIEVE

Have supernatural wonders of God passed away? After His death and resurrection, Jesus told His disciples that miraculous signs and wonders would follow them as they went into the world to preach the gospel (Mark 16:15-18). He was not only speaking to men and women in full time ministry. He was talking to *those who believe*. Do you believe? Jesus was talking to His followers here. The Lord Jesus was speaking to you. He was sending you!

Jesus promised that *anyone* who had faith in Him would do the things He did while on earth. In fact, He said those with faith in Him would do even greater things than He did (John 14:12-14). Praise God! If you have faith in the Lord Jesus Christ He is speaking to you!

God anointed Jesus with the Holy Spirit and with power to do good and to heal all who were oppressed of the devil (Acts 10:38). Jesus was anointed by the Spirit of God to preach good news to the poor, to proclaim freedom for the prisoners, to give sight to the blind, and to release the oppressed (Luke 4:18). Anyone with faith in Jesus will do these things and more! Do you believe?

Jesus was fully divine as the Son of God, yet fully human as Son of man. Jesus' earthly ministry was launched when God anointed Him with the Holy Spirit at the River Jordan. He ministered through the explosive, miracle working power of the Holy Spirit. That same power is available to every Christian who chooses to believe what God instructed him to do under the anointing of His precious Spirit.

We can do nothing by ourselves. We are powerless on our own. But when we go forth with the power and anointing of the Holy Spirit, we carry miracle working, explosive power with us. Yes, with the power of His Spirit, you can do what Jesus did, and more. All for His glory, Halleluia!

## FACT OR TRUTH

It's easy to confess God's healing ability while enjoying perfect health, but what happens when the pain comes, or the symptoms of sickness or disease arrive? What will you proclaim if you receive a bad report from the doctor? Does the bad report from the doctor invalidate God's Word that "by His stripes, you were healed?" (1 Peter 2:24). Does the doctor's report change the will of God from "healing all who are oppressed of the devil" to putting sickness on you instead? No! God doesn't change His mind! *It is His will* for you to enjoy perfect health.

Visible facts often dictate bad reports that are contrary to God's Word. The truth of the Bible is elevated above facts however. Fact and truth are vastly different. For example, it's a fact that our house was once tan in color. When I looked at it, I could see it was obviously tan. That's a fact. We painted our house gray though, then making it a fact that our house is gray. Both facts were true at the time but the facts changed.

Facts can change and be changed. God's Word is truth and cannot change. *God's Word changes facts but facts cannot change God's Word!* We must choose the truth, regardless of what the facts dictate. The truth of the Word of God will set us free.

## JOSHUA AND CALEB

The Report:

Joshua and Caleb, two great men of faith, found an opportunity to demonstrate faith in God's Word. After spies checked out the land God promised to Abraham and his descendants, they returned to the Israelite community with their report. They began by acknowledging the fact that the land was fruitful and flowed with milk and honey. It certainly was fruitful, just as God said. Picture what Numbers 13:23 tells us: "When they reached the Valley of Eshcol, they cut off a branch bearing a single cluster of grapes. Two of them carried it on a pole between them, along with some pomegranates and figs." Imagine! It required two men to carry a single cluster of grapes.

Yes... but...:

But... but... but... Then came the bad report. There were exceptions. The people in Canaan were giants and they were so big and so bad! Certain the giants would overtake them, the faithless Israelites felt unable to enter the Promised Land. Notice the grumbling in Numbers 13:28-33: "But the people who live there are powerful, and the cities are fortified and very large... We can't attack those people; they are stronger than we are... The land we explored devours those living in it. All the people we saw there are of great size... We seemed like grasshoppers in our own eyes, and we looked the same to them."

The report of their discouraging circumstances contradicted God's promise. Unfortunately, instead of trusting the unchanging promise of God, the Israelites chose to trust their circumstances.

Believing the Report of the Lord:

Doubt and unbelief surrounded Joshua and Caleb, yet they refused to believe the bad report. Instead they remained solidly convinced that the report of the Lord was the genuine truth. They knew God had promised them the land; He said the land belonged to them. It was up to them, however, to enter and possess the Promised Land. Refusing to follow the majority opinion, Joshua and Caleb chose to persevere.

In Faith, Not Foolishness:

These tenacious men of faith were not foolish. They didn't deny that there were, in fact, giants in the land, nor did they deny that the giants were big. Joshua didn't say, "Caleb, those giants are just a figment of our imagination. They really don't exist. Even though we see them, they aren't there." Instead of focusing on the giants, however, they focused on God's ability to perform His Word.

Joshua may have asserted, "OK, Caleb, the giants on our property are indeed pretty scary looking. Man, they are big, much bigger and stronger than we are. But it's OK, because God told us the land belonged to us. Don't be afraid of them! Let's go, brother, we can take them on because God is with us."

Joshua and Caleb stood firm! Knowing the land belonged to them, they were convinced they would enter just as God had told them. They were not swayed by doubt and unbelief, even while in the midst of persecution from multitudes of doubters. They knew that although in the natural realm their situation appeared to be contrary to God's Word, God's Word would prevail nevertheless.

According to Scripture, Caleb stood firm and urged, "We should go up and take possession of the land, for we can certainly do it... And do not be afraid of the people of the land, because we will swallow them up. Their protection is gone, but the Lord is with us. Do not be afraid of them" (Numbers 13:30-14:9). Instead of trusting the bad report, they trusted God, because they knew God was a God of His Word.

Faith Made the Way for Entrance into the Promised Land:

Joshua and Caleb were the only two from that generation who

entered and possessed the Promised Land. They were the only two who dared to believe God. The doubters, the ones refusing to believe God's promise, died off in the desert one by one, never getting the opportunity to enjoy the blessings of the Promised Land. The doubters missed God's best.

How many people today are missing out on God's best because they believe the wrong report? How many of God's children miss out on the abundant life because they refuse to believe God's Word? How many never possess the promised land because they focus on the giants in their life instead of on the faithful One who gave them life?

## CALLING THINGS THAT ARE NOT
## AS THOUGH THEY ARE

Have you received a bad report from the doctor? If sickness has crept into your body, don't deny the facts of the report. God doesn't expect you to foolishly deny that sickness exists if it really does exist. He doesn't want you to lie.

God calls things that are not as though they were (Romans 4:17), not things that are as though they are not. In other words, it does no good to repeat over and over, "I don't have cancer, I don't have cancer, I don't have cancer," if the doctor's report indicates you've been diagnosed with cancer. That is calling something that is (cancer) as though it is not. Denying facts will not set you free.

Believing and confessing God's Word over your situation will set you free. Believing and confessing, "By His stripes, I am healed," when the report says you have cancer is calling those things that are not (health) as though they are. The facts may indicate you have an illness but the truth of God's Word says you are healed! Let the Word of God change the report of the doctor instead of letting the report change God's Word.

Refusing to acknowledge the facts of the doctor's report is not only foolish, but dangerous as well. Follow the instructions of your doctor! God uses doctors and medical science as one of many methods to bring physical healing. As you follow the doctor's instructions though, look to the Great Physician and confess and put your faith in God's promises for health. God is faithful to fulfill every promise.

Is your faith in the wrong report? Are you focussed on a bad report, overdrawn checkbook, rocky circumstances, or painful symptoms instead of on the unchanging Word of God?

## OTHER EXAMPLES OF FAITH IN ACTION

Numerous Biblical examples demonstrate God's supernatural miracles. What caused many of those miracles to manifest? Jesus said *faith* prompted the miracles. Let's take a peek at a few examples of miracle working faith.

Woman with the Issue of Blood:

Do you remember the woman who had been subject to bleeding for twelve years? (Mark 5:25). Suffering greatly from a debilitating health issue, she had spent all of her money on medical care, yet instead of getting better she grew even worse. After hearing about Jesus, faith rose and changed her life forever.

As the faith-filled woman approached Jesus and touched the edge of his cloak, she said to herself, "If I just touch His clothes, I will be healed" (Mark 5:28). Touching Him in faith, her bleeding stopped immediately!

Realizing power had gone out from him, Jesus asked who had touched him. Jesus recognized the woman's faith as she explained what she had done. Jesus said, "Daughter, *your faith* has healed you. Go in peace and be free from your suffering" (Mark 5:34).

People were crowding against Jesus that day, so obviously this woman was not the only one who touched Him. Her touch was unique. She touched Jesus in faith, expecting to be healed.

Notice Jesus did not lay hands on her, nor did he even pray for her. Healing flowed from Him when she touched Him in faith. Jesus said *her* faith healed her!

The Two Blind Men:

Let's consider the two blind men seeking the healing hand of Jesus in Matthew 9:27-30. As Jesus went on from there, two blind men followed him, calling out, "Have mercy on us, Son of David!"

When he had gone indoors, the blind men came to him, and he

asked them, "Do you believe that I am able to do this?"

"Yes, Lord," they replied.

Then he touched their eyes and said, "According to your faith will it be done to you;" and their sight was restored. They expected a miracle from God and according to their faith, it was granted!

What are you putting your faith in? Are you expecting God's promises or that which is contrary to God's promises? *According to your faith will it be done to you.*

Blind Bartimaeus:

Blind Bartimaeus called on Jesus for healing and persisted even when many tried to silence him. His persistence paid off. When Jesus finally called for Bartimaeus and asked him what he wanted, Bartimaeus told Jesus he wanted his eyesight restored. He immediately received his miracle. Why? Because of his faith!

"'Go,' said Jesus, 'your faith has healed you.' Immediately he received his sight and followed Jesus along the road" (Mark 10:52). Bartimaeus' faith brought the healing. He dared to believe!

People refusing to believe God's willingness to heal may try to silence you as some tried to silence Bartimaeus. If anyone tries to squelch your faith in the Great Physician, ignore the voice of doubt and unbelief and continue to call out to Jesus with persistence as Bartimaeus did. Faith moves God's healing hand!

Abraham, the Father of Faith:

Abraham, the Father of Faith, obviously stretched his faith to believe he would be the father of many nations (Genesis 15) as God had said. In the natural, becoming the father of many nations, or even the father of one child, was impossible.

Notice Abraham recognized the facts in the natural but chose to believe the Word of the Lord: "Against all hope, Abraham in hope believed and so became the father of many nations, just as it had been said to him, 'So shall your offspring be.' Without weakening in his faith, *he faced the fact that his body was as good as dead – since he was about a hundred years old – and that Sarah's womb was also dead. Yet he did not waver through unbelief regarding the promise of God,* but was strengthened in his faith and gave glory to

God, being fully persuaded that God had power to do what he had promised" (Romans 4:18-21).

Abraham was fully persuaded that God was able to fulfill His promise and fully persuaded that God could do the impossible. God came through with flying colors as He always has and always will. God's promise to Abraham didn't come to pass overnight, but it did come to pass, just as God said it would (Genesis 21).

All of these people chose to believe against all odds. They *chose* to believe God.

## FAITH MUST BE BUILT

Reading, meditating on and confessing God's Word are important to knowing God and receiving from God, yet faith will propel you to victory. Exercising faith in God's Word enables God to perform His word in your life.

It takes time to build faith. Can you trust God for a parking spot? Do you believe God will heal your little toe? Praise God, you must start somewhere. Begin at the level of faith you have and build from there. Although you are given a measure of faith, it is your responsibility to develop it. Don't miss the first step though: You must first believe God's Word is the absolute truth.

## A FAITH LESSON

I shivered with excitement when Tom surprised me with tickets to a Mariners baseball game in Seattle. We packed up our three children and set our course for the Kingdome with snacks in hand and great expectation in our spirits. Although not fond of sports, I was tickled to have an opportunity to see our children enjoy their first baseball game. A faith lesson awaited me at the stadium.

A mouthwatering aroma of juicy hot dogs and salted peanuts enveloped us as we made our way to our seats. As we settled into our chairs, the competing teams warmed up on the field, both expecting to score a win for their team.

The aura of childlike glee was abruptly squelched when I overheard a conversation between some men seated behind us. As their discussion burst forth with inappropriate foul words I cupped my hands over my children's innocent ears in a futile attempt to protect them from this foreign language.

My frustration intensified as their conversation grew increasingly louder and their words gained negative momentum. *How could these people be talking like that?* I sneered to myself, *when they can see there are small children right in front of them!*

I couldn't resist the temptation to turn around to see whom these words were coming from. Trying to be subtle, I spun around only to discover a row of scruffy men guzzling beer. *Oh boy, I can see we're in for a real treat today*, I grumbled and turned around stiffly in my seat.

We stood to our feet to sing the national anthem, which was followed by an astounding display of fireworks. The kids were mesmerized by the flair of color and light. The announcer received a grand applause when he told the crowd that the fireworks would be displayed every time the Mariners got a homerun. That news brought gleeful shouts from our own family cheering section. Our expectant children wanted endless homeruns, hoping to witness a continuous colorful blast of fireworks.

After a roar of encouragement from the crowd, we settled back into our seats to watch the game. Joe, only one year old at the time, was feeling frisky and had a difficult time sitting still. Staring curiously at the strange characters behind us, he appeared to be amused by these loud men, shooting continuous bright smiles at them through the bottle of juice hanging from his mouth.

Although I attempted to ignore the distractions behind us, I couldn't avoid hearing the shouts and obscenities intensify as the game continued. Our irritating neighbors were obviously disgusted with the performance of our team and made it known to anyone within earshot.

I continued to grumble under my breath as my blood pressure increased. I desperately wanted to silence these ignorant men, but couldn't find the right words to put an end their foul talk. I silently asked God to give me the proper words to speak to these fellows. Being keenly aware that the hostile words in my mouth were not from God, I begrudgingly chose to keep my mouth closed.

Inning after inning passed with no score. The men behind us displayed mounting irritation with the Mariners' lack of a successful hit. As one stood up to shout and shake his fist at the team, his beer toppled over, spilling on his shoes and on the floor beneath him. I looked down in disbelief, watching the beer trickle down to our level, saturating my purse that sat underneath my seat. *How disgusting*, I thought to myself. *What next?*

I would have been thrilled had Tom suggested we leave the game early but he was enjoying himself, oblivious to the distractions I couldn't seem to shake. He and our oldest son, James, seemed to be enjoying some special father/son time together. I realized this was a trial I had to work through on my own.

Our three-year-old daughter, Emily, had her mind stayed on the fireworks display she had seen earlier. She desperately wanted to see the fireworks show once again and was growing impatient and disgruntled. Her patience depleted, she couldn't resist the temptation to begin a whining session. "I want to see the fireworks, mommy," she complained and stomped her feet. "I want to see them right now!"

Sensing mounting stress, I explained to Emily that the fireworks couldn't be displayed until our team made a home run. This explanation soothed her for only a moment before she started whining once again.

Sitting in my beer-soaked environment, frustrated at my less than desirable surroundings, I found myself feeling anything but Christian. My patience had worn thin, and I couldn't bear to hear one more complaint from my strong-willed daughter or our drunken neighbors.

Gritting my teeth at Emily's final complaint and request for fireworks, I resisted the temptation to lose my temper and leaned over, whispering firmly in her ear. "OK, Emily, I know you want to see some fireworks again, but they will *not* be displayed again until our team gets a home run. Why don't we pray and ask God to give our team a home run and then you can see your precious fireworks, OK?"

Although my suggestion to Emily was halfhearted on my part, I felt I had successfully put her off a bit longer. It was the ninth inning, so I was thankful this negative experience was almost over.

My less than genuine suggestion did not put Emily off but instead brought a bright smile to her face. Welcoming the idea of asking God for help, she clasped my hands, closed her eyes and petitioned, "Dear God, I want to see the fireworks and I can't see them unless our team gets a home run. Please make our team get a home run. Thank you, God. In Jesus' Name, Amen." Emily sat back in her chair, seemingly satisfied with her prayer and appearing to have no further concern about the fireworks.

In utter disbelief I witnessed the next batter from our team step up to the plate to prepare for the pitch. There were two men already on base. Swinging the bat on the first pitch, he slammed a home run right over the fence!

The bold music played a joyous song as an atmosphere of victory swept across the stadium. Off went the blazing fireworks display as the fans cheered. My mouth hung open as I watched the batter run the bases. We scored three runs.

Emily jumped up and down excitedly as she watched her coveted fireworks. She wasn't the slightest bit surprised that the batter had made that home run. She only enjoyed receiving the answer that God had given her. She'd had a request, made it known to God, and then, sitting back with no further anxiety, had trusted that God would take care of her need. She had prayed in faith and believed God would move on her behalf. I, on the other hand, sat in amazement at the miracle resulting from a simple and childlike prayer.

God gave me a valuable lesson in faith. A child trusts God without cluttering up his mind with reasoning, analyzing and doubting. God showed Himself strong on behalf of Emily, a little child whose heart was loyal to him.

In the middle of an environment filled with foul-mouthed, beer guzzling fans, in the midst of a less than desirable attitude on my part, God moved. God moved powerfully on the baseball field in honoring the prayer of a small child with a simple request. "I tell you the truth, anyone who will not receive the kingdom of God like a little child will never enter it." (Mark 10:15). Do you have faith as a little child?

Faith pleases God. Without faith, it is *impossible* to please God (Hebrews 11:6) God seeks faithful ones that dare to believe His Word even when natural circumstances appear contrary to His promises. Trusting feelings, emotions, or circumstances squelches faith and limits God.

Do you want to please God? Put your faith in Him and His revealed Word. God delights when you trust Him with childlike faith and take Him at His Word.

## LACK OF FAITH HINDERS THE MIRACULOUS

Absolutely nothing is impossible with God (Luke 1:37). *NOTHING!* His arm is not too short to make the impossible possible. Glory to God, He is faithful to do what He promised to do. God wants to pour endless blessings into your life, *if only you can believe.* Can you believe for the impossible or will your unbelief tie God's hands?

Jesus was unable to perform any great miracles in His own hometown. Why? It was not because He did not possess the ability to perform miracles, nor because He willed for the people to remain sick and oppressed. The reason Jesus did few miracles was because of the people's lack of faith. It was *their* lack of faith (Matthews 13:58).

You must be fully persuaded of God's ability to perform His Word as Abraham was, before you can exercise faith to believe and receive God's promises. Can you dare to believe God's Word to you? The blessings of God are hinged to your faith in His Word.

## HOLD TIGHT TO THE TRUTH

As a child, I relished in playing tug of war with a pudgy little puppy. I enticed him to play by waving a toy in front of his face until he couldn't resist sinking his teeth into it. The mighty tug of war was on.

I yanked and pulled one direction as he yanked and pulled the other direction. I tried to pry the toy out of his mouth with all my might, but he continued to hang on, planting his feet into the ground and dragging along as I pulled.

As a last attempt to get the toy away from him, I pulled it straight up into the air. Determined to hang on, his chubby body rose from the ground and dangled in the air with the toy still clenched in his teeth. His perseverance brought him the victory.

Like my little puppy, we need solid determination to stand firm on the Word of God without letting go. When challenging circumstances tempt us to surrender, we must persevere by holding tight to the truth of God's Word. Perseverance will lead to victory (Hebrews 10:36). Grab hold and don't let go until you see the blessing!

## WRITE THE WORD OF GOD
## ON THE TABLET OF YOUR HEART

A prosperous life is clearly dependent on your connection to God and His Word. Psalm 1:1-3 says, "Blessed is the man who does not walk in the counsel of the wicked or stand in the way of sinners or sit in the seat of mockers. But his delight is in the law of the Lord, and on his law he meditates day and night. He is like a tree planted by the streams of water, which yields its fruit in season and whose leaf does not wither. Whatever he does prospers." Moses also tells us that prosperity and success comes by keeping God's Word in our mouth, meditating on it day and night, and being careful to do everything written in it (Joshua 1:8).

Making God's Word a part of your innermost being will enable you to boldly speak victory directly into the midst of your most challenging circumstances. The light of the spoken Word transforms even the worst circumstances. As you speak forth the Word, you create an atmosphere of faith that dispels the darkness. A supernatural, bondage-breaking power bursts forth in the spoken Word. Regardless of what your circumstances dictate, God's Word is powerful and will prevail!

When the Lord prompted me to memorize Scripture several years ago, my first reaction was, "You've got to be kidding. My memory is anything but dependable!" Acting out of obedience, I got started. I wrote a Scripture reference on one side of a 3x5 recipe card and the Scripture verse on the other side. I studied, meditated on, and spoke it daily.

After memorizing the first verse, I created a similar card for a second verse and confessed both daily. Before long, I had a sizeable stack of several hundred cards. Hopping on my treadmill, I walked several miles as I confessed my Scriptures, getting a spiritual and a physical work out at the same time. What a refreshing!

Make the time to write God's Word on your heart. The Holy Spirit will bring those Scriptures to your remembrance when you need them for your own edification and for ministering to others. The number of verses you memorize is not important, but the amount of faith you put in those verses is crucial, so take time to meditate on and study the verses you memorize. It will enhance your spiritual life by leaps and bounds.

The idea of Scripture memorization may seem overwhelming to you as it did to me in the beginning. Although I have memorized several hundred scripture verses today – I started with *one*. You must start somewhere. Regardless of what you feel your memory capabilities are, you *can* memorize Scripture. You can do *all* things through Christ, including Scripture memorization!

A direct correlation between getting God's Word on the inside of you and the prosperity operating in your life is clear in Psalm 1:1-3 and Joshua 1:8 above. Do you want a prosperous life? Get the Word inside of you!

Writing God's Word on the tablet of your heart enables you to enter and possess the Promised Land by faith. God's promises are yours right now. Can you enter and possess the promises as Joshua and Caleb entered and possessed the Promised Land? Provision for every physical, emotional, spiritual and financial need is available to you. Your part is to believe and receive. Is the Word of God written on the tablet of your heart?

## LACK OF KNOWLEDGE

Tom and I once had a craving for Chinese food so we ventured out in search of a Chinese buffet. Quickly making my way through the buffet line, I filled my plate with an abundance of food. Although unable to find some of my favorite Chinese dishes, I settled for the less than satisfying available selection of food.

While paying the bill, I noticed two full rows of buffet food located on the other side of aisle from where we were seated. My favorite foods had been hidden from my sight earlier. There they were: The egg rolls I had been craving, the mouth watering sweet and sour chicken, the steaming fried rice and many other Chinese delicacies. Although the best choices were available the whole time,

I missed out because I didn't know they were available to me.

Likewise, many Christians miss out on God's abundant provision of health, prosperity, hope, joy and peace that await them. Although in need of God's provision, they cannot partake of it because they don't know it's available!

Ignorance causes Christians to miss out on God's best. Sickness and disease run rampant in the body of Christ, yet God never intended for His children to be sick. Many believers experience poverty and depression, yet God provided joy and prosperity through the cross. Lack of knowledge steals His blessings (Hosea 4:6).

In order to have faith for God's provision, you must know it's available to you. If you don't know God provided for your health, how can you possibly have faith for healing? If you don't know He provided for your needs, how can you believe for your provision?

God offers His promises to you as gifts. Do you remember the bag of groceries I bought for my starving neighbor? He had to receive my gift, look in the bag to see what foods were there and then eat them in order to live.

It's up to you to receive the gifts God provided for you as well. Look inside the Word; become fully persuaded of what God gave His Son's life for. Jesus paid a big price for the many benefits He offers, but it is your responsibility to receive those benefits by faith. Have you missed out on the benefits because you haven't discovered they are available to you?

## YOU MUST DISCOVER THE TRUTH FOR YOURSELF

To become fully persuaded that God's Word is the unchanging, forever settled truth, you must discover God's teachings for yourself through personal study of His Word. By automatically accepting everything you hear, without studying or meditating on it yourself, you risk putting your faith in wrong doctrine.

After I fully committed my life to the Lord, I read the Bible from cover to cover. When I reached the end of the Bible for the first time, I realized that my foundation of faith was not built on the truth of God's Word. I had learned man's ways and traditions, yet missed out on God's truth because my faith was not based in the truth of the Bible. What is your faith based on?

## TWISTING AND PERVERTING SCRIPTURE
## LEADS TO DESTRUCTION

If a charismatic man suddenly appeared on earth, performing miraculous signs and wonders, how many Christians would follow him? If one claiming to be Jesus Christ started raising people from the dead, bringing cripples out of wheelchairs and walking on water, how many Christians would think the return of Jesus had arrived? Probably many.

The Bible says, "At that time if anyone says to you, 'Look, here is the Christ!' or 'There he is!' Do not believe it. For false Christs and false prophets will appear and perform great signs and miracles to deceive even the elect – if that were possible" (Matthew 24:24).

Do Christians know how Jesus plans to return? Many don't have a clue. 1 Thessalonians 4:15-17 says, "According to the Lord's own word, we tell you that we who are still alive, who are left till the coming of the Lord, will certainly not precede those who have fallen asleep. For the Lord himself will come down from heaven, with a loud command, with the voice of the archangel and with the trumpet call of God, and the dead in Christ will rise first. After that, we who are still alive and are left will be caught up together with them in the clouds to meet the Lord in the air. And so we will be with the Lord forever."

Those truths may come as a surprise to some, yet in order to be kept from deception, these truths must be known. If false Christs and false prophets have the ability to deceive even God's people, the elect, how can Christians protect themselves from these deceptions?

Jesus said, "If you hold to my teaching, you are really my disciples. Then you will know the truth, and the truth will set you free" (John 8:31-32). We need *knowledge of the truth* to keep us from being duped by deceptive teachings.

People are often deceived by warped or perverted doctrine – even Christians are vulnerable to deception. It is critical for followers of Christ to know the truth of the Bible! If we are familiar with the truth, we can naturally identify the counterfeit when it shows up.

When Jesus was tempted by the devil in the desert, Satan used the Word of God in an attempt to get Jesus to fall. The devil quoted Scripture to Jesus, but twisted it in an attempt to accomplish his goal. Likewise, if someone searches hard enough, he can likely find a Scripture taken out of context to justify sin, then build a doctrine around it. We must study the entire Word of God, know God's nature, and rely on the Holy Spirit for discernment.

When the devil and his cohorts arrive on the scene to deceive, they don't announce their presence with bells and whistles, saying, "Here I am! I'm a false teacher and I'm here to deceive you." Instead, they subtly and deceitfully take unsuspecting people off course bit by bit. If we allow ourselves to stray even a bit off course, we eventually find ourselves heading in the wrong direction, unable to recognize the truth.

Before the return of Christ, false prophets will come in sheep's clothing, yet inside are ferocious wolves (Matthew 7:15). If we judge these false teachers and prophets by their attractive outside appearance, their charisma or their incredible miracles, we risk deception. Their teachings must withstand the scrutiny of the Word of God.

To stay on course, one must know and stand firm on God's Word. Straying outside the teaching of the Bible invites deception. Although many teachings sound good and make us feel good because they tickle our ears, they aren't necessarily the truth. The Apostle Paul sounds the warning: "For the time will come when men will not put up with sound doctrine. Instead, to suit their own desires, they will gather around them a great number of teachers to say what their itching ears want to hear. They will turn their ears away from the truth and turn aside to myths" (2 Timothy 4:3-4). To avoid deception, we must test *everything* by the truth of the Bible.

A woman once shared an experience of being led astray by the deceptive tactics of the evil one. The leadership of a church she had attended introduced the practice of dancing in the spirit. "I felt there was scriptural justification for this," she confessed. "The Bible talks about David dancing, so I willingly accepted it."

The atmosphere of the church subtly began to change. Dancing in the spirit became dancing with partners in the spirit. Dancing with partners became dancing with other people's spouses. Finally, sexual immorality plagued the congregation. What was the result? Broken marriages, broken families, and an empty church with closed doors.

She tearfully admitted, "The subtle deception and changes seemed close enough to the truth to accept as the truth."

Endless opportunities for deception exist through teachings and groups subtly contradicting or perverting the Bible. Many ungrounded Christians fall prey to this deception. Lack of knowledge of God's Word gives the destroyer access to deceive you. Don't open the door to deception even a crack. Stay in the Word.

## THE BIBLE IS THE UNCHANGING ROADMAP TO THE TRUTH

People, relationships, emotions, doctrines and circumstances change. God, and His Word, however, *never* change (Malachi 3:6). We are on solid foundation when we stand on God's Word. When all else fails, when all else is uncertain and shaky, we can trust the unfailing truth. There are no surprises with God. What He did in the past, He will do now. The Bible explodes with revelation truth for yesterday, today and forever.

The Bible is the roadmap to mark our path on the journey in Christ Jesus. His infallible Word directs us toward our Christian destination. By absorbing and putting our faith in God's Word, we will discover the abundant Christian life along the way.

Search your heart and settle the issue of whether or not you will take God at His Word once and for all. If you do not settle it, you will be tossed to and fro and will waver in your faith whenever circumstances get tough.

Do you believe the Word of God? Do you believe *the entire* Word of God? Settle it now.

# CHAPTER 6
# To Obey Or Not To Obey –
# That Is The Question

## OBEDIENCE MATTERS

Demand for obedience echoes into all seasons of life. Parents instruct us to obey, teachers demand obedience, we're required to obey authority figures and must obey governmental law. God Himself expects us to obey Him and His Word. Obedience matters to God and is required by God.

## ARE YOU A HEARER OR A DOER?

As we learn God's plan by studying His Word, we face continual opportunities to apply the truth of His Word into our lives. Studying the Bible is not enough to produce a fruitful Christian life. Hearing the Word of God is not enough either. We must learn what God's Word says and then act on that knowledge through obedience. If we hear God's Word, yet don't practice it, the Bible says we deceive ourselves (James 1:22). Ouch!

Hearing, meditating on, and confessing God's Word are critical. If we do not feed our spirit with the Word of God, we starve spiritually. But if we hear, meditate on and confess God's Word without obedience, it benefits us little. James 1:23-25 explains this truth: "Anyone who listens to the word but does not do what it says is like a man who looks at his face in a mirror and, after looking at himself, goes away and immediately forgets what he looks like. But the man who looks intently into the perfect law that gives freedom, and continues to do this, not forgetting what he has heard, but doing it – he will be blessed in what he does."

Practicing God's Word enables you to discover your true reflection in Christ. When you look in your spiritual mirror, do you see Jesus? If you are a doer of the Word of God, you will see His reflection.

A Christian commonly rejoices after hearing a powerful message preached from the pulpit. Maybe the anointed message illuminated exactly what he needed to overcome a spiritual struggle. The pastor surely "read his mail" so to speak. What happens next? Will he choose to meditate on and apply that Word to his life or will he forget the message by the next day?

Excitement about God's Word is not enough to bring positive change to your life. An emotional experience is not enough to bring change either. You must hear the Word *and* be a doer of the Word to discover victorious living on your journey in Christ.

## OBEDIENCE IS A CHOICE

Obedience to God is not automatic and does not happen by accident. Obedience is a willful decision, one that is seldom easy. Endless opportunities to obey or disobey God are scattered along the path of your Christian journey. What will you choose?

When our son Joseph was three years old, we lived near a busy street. Because I love Joseph and want to ensure his safety, I took him outside to show him the boundaries of the yard. After encouraging him to enjoy the toys, swing set and other provisions within the boundaries of our yard, I warned him of the dangers lurking beyond the boundaries. Pointing out the cars driving by, I explained he could be hurt by oncoming traffic if he stepped out of the limitations I set, even if only for a moment. He would remain in safety if he obeyed, but risked danger if he disobeyed.

In a similar way, God clearly expressed His desires for us and from us through His Word. He set boundaries, so to speak, which we must stay within if we want to receive the fullness of His provision. If we choose to step out of those boundaries, into disobedience, we place ourselves in potential danger. Disobedience to God places us in the devil's territory.

The choice is ours. We can live God's way, flourishing under the shadow of His wing, or our way. We enjoy the privilege of making our own choices and the privilege of reaping the consequences of those choices. Simply put: good choices produce good consequences, bad choices produce bad consequences.

The concept of obedience is familiar even to a small child. If a child obeys, he receives rewards of praise or goodies. If he disobeys, he faces a spanking or other type of discipline. Just as children face consequences for obedience or disobedience to their parents, we also face consequences for obedience and disobedience to God.

Following God's plan produces abundant blessings. Many of His promises are conditional though. You can't receive God's best while disobeying Him at the same time. His blessings are poured out on you *if* you obey the Lord and His commands. "If" is a little word with significant weight as you can see in Deuteronomy 28:1-13:

> *If you fully obey the Lord your God* and carefully follow all his commands I give you today, the Lord your God will set you high above all the nations on earth. All these blessings will come upon you and accompany you *if you obey* the Lord your God: You will be blessed in the city and blessed in the country. The fruit of your womb will be blessed, and the crops of your land and the young of your livestock – the calves of your herds and the lambs of your flocks. Your basket and your kneading trough will be blessed. You will be blessed when you come in and blessed when you go out. The Lord will grant that the enemies who rise up against you will be defeated before you. They will come at you from one direction but flee from you in seven. The Lord will send a blessing on your barns and on everything you put your hand to. The Lord your God will bless you in the land he is giving you... The Lord will grant you abundant prosperity – in the fruit of your womb, the young of your livestock and the crops of your ground – in the land he swore to your forefathers to give you. The Lord will open the heavens, the storehouse of his bounty, to send rain on your land in season and to bless all the work of your hands. You will lend to many nations but will borrow from none. The Lord will make you the head, not the tail. *If you pay attention to the commands of the Lord your God* that I give you this day and carefully follow them, you will always be at the top, never at the bottom.

God's blessings are rich! Following God's commands causes everything you do to prosper! Praise the Lord!

If these blessings are available, then why are they absent in many Christians' lives? Sadly Christians often want the blessings of God but are unwilling to obey what God asks of them. God's plan does not bless disobedience.

Imagine the hoard of spoiled brats God would have on His hands if His children continually received His blessings, yet had no accountability to obedience. The blessings of God are released through obedience. Are you willing to obey? As you obey, you position yourself to receive God's very best.

Part of maturing spiritually is choosing to apply the revelation of God's Word by obeying whatever He asks of you. Although revelation knowledge is not gained overnight, you can apply what you know until God opens your eyes to more revelation. Growth comes step by step and day by day. You build precept upon precept.

You are accountable for what you know. For example, a baby Christian with no knowledge of God's desire for him to tithe is not in willful disobedience if he fails to tithe. A mature Christian, however, who has heard and understands God's requirement in tithing, yet refuses to obey, is in willful disobedience. Christian friend, once you know what God wants from you, you can't claim ignorance. Discover freedom and liberty as you submit yourself to God, determined to obey everything He asks of you.

Change often becomes necessary when you choose to be wholly submitted to God. Determination to submit and commit to God's plan impacts how quickly those changes take place. The quicker you conform to God's Word, the sooner you receive the benefits of obedience. Delaying obedience delays God's best.

## THE DEVIL ENCOURAGES DISOBEDIENCE

The devil cringes when Christians purpose to obey God. When you choose to obey God, Satan will try to find out just how serious your commitment is. Satan will tempt you with alternatives and compromises in an effort to thwart your decision of obedience.

Let's look at the area of tithing as an example. Maybe you want to obey God by tithing, but feel you can't afford to tithe. Maybe your unpaid debts help you justify disobedience. If you delay obedience to God's instruction, the devil will make certain you can never afford to tithe. Are you planning to wait until you can afford to tithe? If so, you likely never will. Disobedience places you in the devil's territory where he can steal your money. Obedience brings God on the scene where He will rebuke the devourer for you! (Malachi 3:11).

Choose to obey God and leave the rest up to Him. Obedience ushers in the divine hand of God. Honor God and His Word first and He will honor His Word and His promises to you. God is faithful!

## CONFIDENCE IN THE PROMISES THROUGH OBEDIENCE

Obedience to God brings confidence that God hears your prayers and answers according to His promises. When an obedient child of God approaches God's throne, he doesn't need to whimper with his tail between his legs in meager hope that God might answer him. He can have confidence! He can expect God to move on his behalf!

1 John 5:14-15 says, "This is the confidence we have in approaching God: that if we ask anything according to his will, he hears us. And if we know that he hears us – whatever we ask – we know we have what we asked of him." When you ask according to God's will, Halleluia, you can *know* you will have it… *if* you are obedient.

It is God's will that you walk in health and enjoy a prosperous life. Since God's will is His Word, you can expect to see those blessings operating in your life. That is shouting ground! Hallelujah! You cannot, however, claim and stand on the promises of God if you do not meet His conditions. Willful disobedience steals confidence because it takes you out of God's will. You must meet God's conditions before you can have confidence in receiving His promises.

## LIFE OF OBEDIENCE WORKS –
## OCCASSIONAL OBEDIENCE DOESN'T

Obedience to God is not something to try, but the standard to live by. If we merely "try it out," we will not find victory in the long run. We will be unable to stand firm until the end if we obey God only when positive circumstances make it easy to obey.

Without a doubt, you will face trials. You may have seasons of trial when all you have left to stand on are God's promises. Obedience to God enables you to stand confidently in the midst of a torrential storm, knowing God will move on your behalf.

God searches for opportunities to move on behalf of those who are faithful to Him, praise God! Let Him find you faithful. 2 Chronicles 16:9 says, "For the eyes of the Lord run to and fro throughout the whole earth, to show Himself strong on behalf of those whose heart is loyal to him" (NKJV). What about you? Are you loyal to Him?

A consistent life of obedience positions you to receive God's finest blessings. When you are in right standing with God through obedience, He will pass over multitudes to search you out in order to fulfill what He promised to you. Halleluia, expect the victory!

## LOVING GOD MEANS OBEYING GOD

Obedience to God demonstrates love for God. Jesus said that if we love Him, we will obey what He commands (John 14:15 and 1 John 5:3). Do you love God enough to do what He says? Do you love Him enough to obey Him?

Demonstrate your love for God simply by obeying His Word. Love God by loving others. Love Him by forgiving others. Love God by bringing your tithes and offerings to Him. Love Him by doing *all* He asks of you.

1 John 2:3-6 says, "We know that we have come to know him if we obey his commands. The man who says, 'I know him,' but does not do what he commands is a liar, and the truth is not in him. But if anyone obeys his word, God's love is truly made complete in him. This is how we know we are in him: Whoever claims to live in him must walk as Jesus did." Do you love God? If the answer is "yes," you must do what He commanded. Love and obedience go hand in hand. To love God and know God you must obey God.

## DOES A LITTLE COMPROMISE REALLY MATTER?

Does obedience to God really matter? Won't God understand if we occasionally disobey as long as we can justify our actions? Do not be deceived! Compromise leads to moral deterioration and produces seared consciences that cannot recognize right from wrong.

Compromising values not only affects our relationship with God, but affects the people observing our actions as well. Children commonly observe adults compromising the very values they teach in the home. The strongest message adults send to children is through actions, not words.

A common area of compromise, even within the body of Christ is the issue of honesty. Does God require us to be honest with the little things? Do we have to obey God's command to tell the truth? Do those little white lies really count?

My husband and I once packed up our three children and our daughter's eight-year-old friend whom I'll call Mary, and headed for an amusement park adventure in Northern Idaho. Our mini van was plump with excitement as we set our course for a day of roller coasters, fun and food. Mary chattered endlessly about the special treats she planned to buy with her money.

Although our family had season passes, we took our place in a long line to purchase a ticket for our little friend, Mary. Mary's bright smile turned to a frown when she noticed the admission prices: General admission for age 8 and above – $23.99; Under 8 – $15.99. With only $23.00 in her pocket, Mary's plan for treats was about to be squelched.

When I told Mary that she had to pay full admission to get into the park, she piped up, "No I don't, we can just tell them I'm seven. I'm little so they'll believe I'm only seven." She obviously thought her solution would solve her money problems and was oblivious to the fact that she was compromising the truth.

I bent down to her level and explained that it would be dishonest to tell them she was seven when she was really eight. "We have to tell the truth," I insisted, leaving no room for compromise. Startled by my refusal to go along with her plan, Mary surrendered only because she had no choice.

Straightening back up, I immediately noticed a woman walking across the parking lot in our direction. Although many other people filled the ticket line, the woman stopped at our spot, as if she had chosen us out of the line. "We purchased advance discount tickets for our group," she said. "And a couple of people cancelled at the last minute." Wondering why she was sharing her dilemma with us, it became clear when she continued. "The park management suggested we try to sell our extra tickets. Do you by chance need a ticket? I'll sell it to you for $14."

I happily took her up on her offer, realizing the ticket she offered was even less than a ticket would cost if Mary had lied about her age. Doing a quick calculation, Mary realized she had more than enough to buy her special treats after all. The sparkle in her eyes told me she wondered if I had prearranged the ticket line scene just to teach her a lesson. I hadn't prearranged it, but I knew the One who did. Honesty opened the door for a blessing from heaven. I looked up and smiled, knowing we had witnessed a God-ordained lesson that was now frozen in the memory of a child.

How many eight-year-old "seven-year-olds" pass through the gates of amusements parks around the world every day? Probably many. How many parents are right beside their children, willing to compromise the truth to save a few dollars? Honesty is an endangered species causing the moral fiber of society to unravel out of control. Are adults leading the future generation into moral destruction through their demonstration of disobedience to God?

The world's voice says, "So what's the big deal if I say she's younger than she really is?" … "So what if I didn't pay for that item. It was in the bottom of the basket and the sales clerk didn't see it. It's not my fault." … "Why be concerned because someone gave me too much money back? Heck, I got a good deal!" That little white lie, that compromise of the truth, does it really matter? It matters to God.

If we dust off the Ten Commandments that society tries so hard to bury we will find they are the same as they were when Moses brought them down from Mount Sinai. Inscribed by the finger of God, the eighth command was written, "You shall not give false testimony against your neighbor" (Exodus 20:16).

Adult's actions often speak so loud that children cannot hear their words. Children learn much more from *seeing* honesty demonstrated than from *hearing* about honesty. When adults compromise the truth it sears the conscience of a generation that will soon lead the world. "Do as I say and not as I do" does not work.

Every time an adult pounces on an opportunity to demonstrate honesty and integrity, he stamps morality on a child's conscience. If children see honesty displayed by those in authority over them, eventually they will expect high moral standards as the norm instead of giving a blank stare of disbelief when they see a display of honesty.

Replace "Do as I say and not as I do" with "Do as I do because I do what God says to do." Then the moral decay resulting from compromised values will turn a corner and offer new life to a suffering generation that searches for hope.

Tom and I discovered another opportunity to demonstrate honesty to young eyes when we made a trip to the mall with our son Joseph, who was six years old at the time. Two young men pulled up behind us in the parking lot and offered us top quality speakers at a "sweet price." They snickered as they volunteered the reason they had twenty new speakers in their possession. "We went to pick up ten speakers and the idiots gave us ten *pair* of speakers."

After indicating we were not interested in their "sweet deal," we jotted down a description of their van, dialed 911 and reported what we believed to be stolen property.

Regardless of what the truth was behind the speakers, I discovered a diamond in the ruff. In the back seat, Joseph had been quietly observing, not realizing he was absorbing part two of a lesson about honesty.

Part one of the honesty lesson occurred on a shopping trip to the grocery store. Joseph and I had planned to buy a box of ice cream sandwiches that was on special. The freezer section had run out of the ice cream, so an employee visited the deep freezer to get more stock for me. I paid for my groceries and we continued on our way.

As I unpacked my groceries at home, I noted that the box of ice cream sandwiches seemed unusually large. Looking closer, I realized the grocer had given me a box containing six individual packages of twelve ice cream sandwiches instead of the one box of twelve I had paid for.

Joseph thought the floodgates of heaven had opened. "Cool, Mom, look at all of this ice cream! We can keep it, can't we? It was their mistake. It's not our fault they gave us too much. Please can we keep it?"

I jumped on the opportunity to demonstrate honesty, explaining that because we had not paid for the ice cream, it did not belong to us. I pointed out that taking advantage of the store's error would be dishonest. We immediately headed back to the store to return the ice cream overage.

Joseph witnessed me explaining my ice cream dilemma three times before the store manager finally understood that I was returning ice cream I had not paid for. With an obvious expression of shock, the manager said, "Wow, thanks for being so honest."

I drove home pondering the manager's reaction of surprise. I certainly would let the store know if they overcharged me, so shouldn't they expect me to let them know if they undercharged me as well? Keeping the ice cream wasn't an option we even considered.

Although Joseph had to watch his coveted ice cream go back to the store, he gained a memory I believe was seared into his conscience. Thanks to our speaker peddlers, he also now understands what lack of integrity means.

The young speaker dealers will eventually learn that it never pays to be dishonest. A clean conscience and right standing with God is worth much more than the short-term financial harvest dishonesty might bring.

We teach children reading, writing and arithmetic, yet the lessons of character often get overlooked. The real 911 emergency is that our society lacks basic godly character traits. Is honesty now the exception and not the norm? How sad.

Obedience is not always the easy choice but is always the right choice. Obedience is a learned behavior. It is not uncommon to wrestle with issues and habits in the process of learning obedience. Some issues may literally be a battle for you; you will have to obey purely by will because your flesh is pulling you in the opposite direction. It's your choice. Facing challenge in obedience is a normal part of growing spiritually.

## WILLING AND OBEDIENT
Examine the attitude of your heart in obedience. The willingness accompanying your obedience impacts the fruit of your obedience.

Isaiah 1:19 says, "If you are willing and obedient, you shall eat the good of the land" (NKJV). *Willing and obedient.* Do a check-up on your heart attitude. Are you obedient, yet your heart is grumbling with an unwilling attitude?

Is your heart cheerful when you give your tithe, or are you daydreaming about the things you wish you could use the money for instead? Are you serving in a ministry, yet moan and complain about it in your heart? Do you feel inconvenienced serving in the body of Christ? Are you serving with the wrong attitude? Are you unwilling and obedient or willing and obedient?

Several years ago, a pastor asked me to teach a fourth grade Sunday School class. I agreed to pray about it. But after praying, I received no direction whatsoever. Although I lacked clear direction from God, I was confident that if I stepped out and taught the class, God would direct me once I was moving. I agreed to teach.

As the class starting date neared, I recognized a wrong attitude in my heart. I worried and fretted about being overloaded in other ministries I was already involved in. Mounting stress about other responsibilities I had already taken on at church, at home, and in the schools enveloped me. *How will I ever find the time to prepare the lessons? One more thing is all I need!* I complained to myself, feeling completely overwhelmed.

Although acting in obedience, I had an unwilling attitude in my heart. With an attitude needing an overhaul, I repented, submitted myself to God and prepared for my class. Because of the change of heart, I anticipated the start date with great expectation.

My Sunday School class brought tremendous blessings and birthed a deep love for those precious children. I treasured the expressions on their faces as God penetrated their hearts through revelation of His Word. I fondly look back on those little kids searching me out for a hug. Without an attitude adjustment, I could not have been used by God to impact those children. Obedience to God, joined with a willingness to obey, released the blessings. Be willing *and* obedient. Attitude matters!

Obedience to God's personal direction is critical. When God speaks, we must listen. When He tells us to act, we must act. If we hesitate, we risk missing out on some incredible, life-changing opportunities to be used by the Master.

God rarely explains His reasoning for asking us to do something for Him. God is not required to explain the details! It is only up to us to obey Him.

My children and I used to collect Beanie Babies, a once popular little stuffed beanbag toy creation. We often had to search for the ones we wanted. On one "Beanie hunt" we found some of the Beanies we had been hunting for. I was fond of one in particular. As we made our beanie choices in the store, I chatted briefly with a woman who was also looking at the Beanies. After paying for the Beanies, we left the store.

As I pulled out of my parking place, I noticed the woman I had talked to coming out of the store. The still, small voice of the Holy Spirit spoke. *Pick out your favorite Beanie Baby* (it was clearly not to be any one, but my favorite one) *and give it to the woman.*

I pulled my favorite Beanie out of the bag, put the van in "park" and told the kids to wait for me. I ran across the parking lot, asked the woman to roll down her window and said, "I know this may sound unusual, but the Lord wants you to have this Beanie Baby. Be blessed." Tears rolled from her eyes as she choked out a "thank you."

I ran back to my van and burst into tears. My children asked me why I was crying; I told them I was just happy. I was crying tears of joy.

Driving home, I pondered the parking lot scene. What had God done? I wondered if the woman had cried out to God that very morning asking Him if He still cared about her? Maybe she didn't know the Lord yet and when she sees the cute little Beanie on her dresser, she'll remember the seed I planted when I told her, "The Lord wants you to have this." God knows why He wanted her to have it. That's really all that matters. We are God's hands, feet, and mouth. Are we willing to obey Him when He asks us to do something for Him?

## HUMBLE YOURSELF AND TURN TO GOD

Have you disobeyed God? Forgiveness awaits you through the blood of Jesus. It's not too late to repent and recommit yourself to a life of obedience. 2 Chronicles 7:14-15 says, "If my people, who are called by my name, will humble themselves and pray and seek my face and turn from their wicked ways, then will I hear from heaven and will forgive their sin and will heal their land. Now my eyes will be open and my ears attentive to the prayers offered in this place."

You can start fresh right now! Before you go any further, I encourage you to purpose in your heart to obey God in everything. A commitment to obey God in everything, without question, will remove the need to struggle through choices of obedience in the future.

To obey or not to obey, that is the question. What do you choose?

# CHAPTER 7
# You Want Me To Give What?

## MINE, MINE, MINE!

While studying the Bible as a new believer, I intentionally glazed over the area of giving. I spent little time meditating on the subject of giving, knowing that if I learned the truth, I would be accountable to obey. I wasn't quite ready to part with *my* money. After all, I liked *my* money. I liked earning *my* money, managing *my* money and spending *my* money. It was *my* money and I wanted control over it. I did not yet realize that "*my*" money was not my money at all. It was God's money, just as everything I had was His. The earth, the world, and everything in it belongs to the Lord (Psalm 24:1).

## THE LOVE OF MONEY

I loved money and coveted material things. Elevating material possessions to a high priority left me spiritually out of balance. The love of money had subtly crept into my life. Although I loved God as a born again believer, my priorities were mixed up. Another area of my life was about to be transformed by renewing my mind to the Word of God.

The love of money is a root of all kinds of evil (1 Timothy 6:10). Money is not the root of evil. The *love of money* is the root of evil. What motivates prostitution? What fuels drug dealers? What lurks behind the schemes and plans of a burglar? The love of money!

Money is obviously a key tool needed to survive on earth, an absolute necessity in life. Without money, we cannot meet our basic needs, bless others, nor preach the gospel to the nations. Some people say, "I just want God to give me enough to get by." This is a self-centered request because if we only have enough money to squeak by, how can we possibly help build an orphanage, finance a ministry or give to the poor? To accomplish God's work on earth, we need money.

We are fools if we think we do not need money but bigger fools if we do not keep money in the proper perspective. Our willingness to part with money to fulfill God's purpose on this earth reveals the condition of our heart. Where your treasure is, your heart will be also (Matthew 6:21).

Willingness to give selflessly was an area in which I needed much change. I enjoyed earning and hoarding as much money as possible and considered it a challenge to successfully build and manage my financial accounts. I relished in buying nice things and gloried in paying cash for everything. I pridefully enjoyed giving money or possessions away; as long as it was *my* decision to give. Giving money or material possessions away for God's purpose and plan, however, was foreign to me.

Money had become a god to me. Divine intervention and a willing attitude set me free from material bondage.

## THE TRUTH OF TITHING

Early in our marriage, Tom and I tithed regularly to the church we attended. As new believers, we were unaware that "tithe" actually meant ten percent, so we gave what we felt we could afford to give. Feeling quite proud and puffed up about our "generosity," I dropped our gift in the offering basket every time it came my way. Entering the divine school of giving, I had much to learn.

Uncertain of God's specific expectations in the area of giving, we began searching for answers. Because God made everything else so clear up to this point, we were confident He would bring clarity on the subject of tithing as well.

God immediately began teaching us. Although we had not received scriptural teaching on the tithe, I remembered as a child seeing my dad put his check in the offering basket. Tom and I vaguely recalled hearing that ten percent of our income belonged to God so we decided to practice giving ten percent. *Surely though*, I thought, *God will allow us to give Him ten percent "after" we pay taxes and "after" we pay Tom's child support obligation. Of course,* I reasoned, *We should also deduct the money we give to other ministries outside the church*. I felt it would be unreasonable for God to expect ten percent right off the top as it would cause too much of a financial strain. Even our misguided calculation of ten percent was a huge stretch from where we were starting.

Tom was a natural at giving so our new practice of tithing was not a problem for him. It was a problem for me, however. On the outside my face revealed a smile but inside, I kicked and screamed as I released the check into the basket. *How are we going to make ends meet if we give all of this money away?* I silently fretted. Although we obeyed what we thought God wanted us to do, the attitude of my heart was sour. I was not a cheerful giver.

Finally, surrendering to the undeniable conviction that filled our hearts, we chose to do what we felt in our heart was right. Our conscience cleared and the struggle ended as we determined to give God ten percent right off the top – *before* taxes, *before* child support, *before* other ministry offerings, *before* food or anything else. We put God first.

## A TEST OF OBEDIENCE

Immediately facing a test of obedience, our finances came under fierce attack. An incredible squeeze on our financial status came from all directions the moment we decided to give the first ten percent of our income to the Lord.

Financial difficulties we had never experienced in the past suddenly stared us in the face. The enemy taunted us as he whispered, "Hmm, financial pressure is increasing... Maybe you better not follow through with your commitment to tithe... You'll never meet your needs if you give your firstfruits to God... You better wait."

We considered postponing our decision to tithe, yet could not ignore the solid commitment we had made to obey God. Disobedience simply wasn't an option. Standing firm to honor God first, we blindly trusted Him to work out the financial details.

Swallowing hard, I wrote the first check and dropped it in the basket. Obedience to honor God brought an immediate change to the attitude of my heart. No longer resisting the truth, I obeyed with a cheerful heart.

## WHAT HAPPENS WHEN YOU OBEY IN YOUR GIVING?

From the day we wrote our first tithe check to this day, regardless of where we are or what our financial status is, our tithe always goes to the house of God, without compromise and without excuse. From that day forward, we have lacked for nothing, as God faithfully meets our every need.

As a result of taking the step of obedience, God's divine hand moves miraculously to give us favor in the financial realm. Does financial pressure come? Yes! Has the devil ever tried to steal our money? Of course! But when the devil tries to attack our finances, it is short-lived because he cannot have his way with God's people who obey the King of Kings and Lord of Lords.

When you obey God's Word in giving your tithes and offerings, you can be confident that all of your needs will be met according to His glorious riches (Philippians 4:19). God supernaturally makes a way when there seems to be no way. He lovingly takes care of you even if everything around you is falling apart. He brings abundance when you're surrounded by lack. God is faithful! Obedience to God with your finances, mixed with wisdom in being a good steward with money, results in financial victory.

If you honor God with the first fruits of your increase, the abundance of His blessings will surely flow through your life. It is God's *good pleasure* to bless you and to cause you to prosper! Proverbs 3:9-10 says, "Honor the Lord with your wealth, with the firstfruits of all of your crops; then your barns will be filled to overflowing, and your vats will brim over with new wine." Hallelujah! Notice though, you play an important part in bringing the blessings: You must honor God with the firstfruits of your wealth.

## GOD'S PROMISE IS CONDITIONAL

If you willfully disobey God, you cannot stand on His provisional promises. You cannot pray with confidence and cannot *know* God will meet your financial needs when attacks from the enemy arrive unexpectedly. All you can do if you willfully disobey is hope for the best. If you withhold your tithe, you are in rebellion and have opened the door for Satan to have his way with you.

To expect God to meet your needs, you must meet His condition of giving tithes and offerings first. Malachi 3:8-10 tells us God's conditions in the area of giving: "'Will a man rob God? Yet you rob me. But you ask, 'How do we rob you?' 'In tithes and offerings. You are under a curse – the whole nation of you – because you are robbing me. *Bring the whole tithe into the storehouse that there may be food in my house*." The *whole* tithe, or ten percent. Those are the conditions.

If you obey, you can enter into the blessings of your obedience: "'Test me in this,' says the Lord Almighty, 'and see if I will not throw open the floodgates of heaven and pour out so much blessing that you will not have enough room for it. I will prevent pests from devouring your crops, and the vines in your fields will not cast their fruit,' says the Lord Almighty" (Malachi 3:11). Those are the blessings!

How many pests are devouring believers' possessions because of their disobedience to God in tithes and offerings? Often the financial lack causing them to say, "I can't afford to tithe," is actually a result, in part, of their disobedience to God. They are under a curse and until they honor God with tithes and offerings, they will not get out of the hole they are in. They are putting their money into a purse with holes in it. Disobedience is an open door inviting the devil in to attack and destroy. Don't blame the devil for the consequences of your disobedience.

When you choose to obey God, *He* rebukes the devourer for you, praise God! Dare to obey God and see supernatural miracles happen in your finances. Honor God with the first fruits of your increase and watch the abundance of His blessings flow through your life.

## THE TITHE AND OFFERINGS ARE NOT THE SAME

As clearly stated in Malachi 3:8, the tithe is not the same as the offering. The word "tithe" means ten percent and is the basic minimum requirement. The tithe belongs to God, in the house of God you consider to be your church home. The *first* ten percent of your income belongs to God, not to you.

The tithe is just the beginning however. Offerings in your church home and to outside ministries are over and above the tithe. Although God clearly says that ten percent of your increase is His,

He leaves offerings up to you: You get to determine the recipients and the amount of your offerings. Let Him direct you to good, fertile, fruit-producing soil to sow into.

Are you obeying God with your tithes and offerings? Is the IRS, your medical insurance or your retirement savings plan getting the firstfruits of your increase or is God getting the firstfruits? Is God getting your leftovers? Do you come into God's presence with an acceptable gift or are you empty handed? Have you given God what is His or are you robbing Him?

## GOD DOES NOT NEED YOUR MONEY – HE NEEDS YOUR OBEDIENCE

God does not need your money or your possessions. The Creator of the universe can move money or material things from point A to point B whenever and however He desires to. God will get His work accomplished on the earth with or without your money. God does, however, need your obedience as many of His promises are conditional and fulfillment of those promises is dependent on your obedience.

Do you trust God enough to obey Him or are you afraid you cannot afford to obey? Do you plan to tithe after you get on your feet financially? Are you waiting until your finances turn around? Don't wait! Your obedience will turn your financial lack around!

God already knows about your financial situation. Financial troubles do not invalidate God's Word and do not excuse you from obedience. Trust God enough to obey God and He will work out all details regardless of how impossible they look to you.

If you know what God desires from you, yet choose to disobey, you enter into enemy territory unarmed. Shut the door to the devourer! Slam it shut on the enemy by obeying God.

A Christian will commonly "try" tithing after receiving revelation of God's plan for tithing. "This tithing thing sounds good," he says. "I think I'll try it and see if it works." After a few short months, if his financial dilemmas do not turn around, he often gives up and thinks, "God's Word obviously doesn't work. God said He would pour out so much blessing that I wouldn't have enough room to hold it all... I'm still in debt... creditors are still chasing me... I'm not going to tithe anymore!"

Financial debt is created over a period of time. Getting out of debt takes time as well. The financial situation you live in today is a result of yesterday's choices. God normally does not instantly wipe out a person's debt when he becomes obedient to tithing and giving offerings. Obedience in tithing is not intended to rescue you from your financial troubles. Are you motivated to give only because you want God to bail you out of trouble or are you motivated by your love for God?

Financial victory is not a secret formula. Financial success requires not only obedience to God, but also wisdom in spending, living within your means and being a faithful steward over your money. Have you charged your credit cards to the limit? That is not God's plan for prosperity. God has a better plan.

Obedience to God requires perseverance and diligence. Living according to God's Word for the long haul produces a life of abundance. Victorious Christian living requires a consistent life of obedience, not seasons of obedience.

Be consistent in your obedience to God! If you only obey when it's convenient to obey or when you can afford to obey, you buy a ticket for a spiritual roller coaster ride. Consistent obedience enables you to confidently stand on solid ground. God's ways are to live by, not to try.

## ANOTHER TEST OF OBEDIENCE

We faced another test of obedience when Tom's occupation brought us to Eastern Washington. We asked God for wisdom and were confident we were in the midst of His will. After relocating, however, business income declined rapidly.

The temptation to question God was great: "What's up with this, God? We obeyed you! We followed your direction! Why are our finances going the wrong direction? You said our barns would be full if we tithed and they're not full! Maybe we should quit giving because it looks like God's Word isn't true!"

Overcoming the temptation to doubt, we knew of God's faithfulness to His unchanging Word. Tom remained faithful to his work and to God through some very trying times. His diligence and integrity persevered through a challenging season of testing.

We continued to tithe and give generous offerings although in the natural we were unsure of how we would make ends meet. After nine months of a dry business climate, the situation grew worse. A large percentage of employees were to be laid off and the remaining people, including Tom, were required to take an automatic ten percent pay cut.

We persevered and continued in faithful obedience to God. Although we did not understand why we faced these challenging circumstances, peace enveloped us, as we knew God would somehow turn our circumstances around. Instead of looking at our natural circumstances, we gazed at the promises of God. We stood firm, expecting God to move on our behalf, and were confident He would honor His promises because we had obeyed Him.

The same week the layoffs and pay cuts arrived, Tom received an unexpected phone call. Tom's previous employer of 20 years needed his expertise in a unique position with the company. Although Tom had left the organization for a position with another company two years earlier, his reputation of integrity and diligence continued to linger from various locations within the company. God's favor surrounded Tom like a shield.

Tom accepted the new position, which included a significant increase and many benefits we had lived without for the past two years. Obedience and perseverance made the way for us to stand firm throughout this extended time of testing. God faithfully brought the victory. He is *always* faithful!

Your obedience will be challenged and tested as well. Continue to obey God in giving even when in the midst of financial challenges. Obedience propels you through the press of testing to victory every time. God fulfills His promises. He *always* fulfills His promises, but you must persevere through obedience.

## OBEDIENCE CLOSES THE DOOR TO THE ENEMY

Maybe you feel it isn't necessary to obey God in the arena of tithes and offerings because you already enjoy financial prosperity. You are unstable if your faith is in your job or in your current financial status. Putting your faith in the stability of your job or career instead of in God puts you on a shaky foundation. Your soaring career or fat bank account could fizzle overnight due to circumstances beyond your control. What will you stand on then?

Satan is a destroyer. He can and will do anything within his power to steal from you if the door is opened to him. He forever searches for ways to worm into your life. If you willfully disobey God, you invite the evil one in to bring destruction in your finances. Schemes of the devil can wreak havoc on your finances and your stability. Financial ruin and poverty is one of Satan's specialties.

Obedience to God assures divine protection from the enemy's schemes. Your obedience to God makes a way for you to press through what appears to be hopeless circumstances and into the victory. God will deal with Satan on your behalf! ...if you have obeyed (Malachi 3:11).

If you feel you cannot afford to obey God, may I suggest you cannot afford not to obey? Obedience puts you on solid ground where nothing can harm you. God honors His promises and honors your obedience to Him.

## WHY DON'T MORE CHRISTIANS GIVE?

Is it difficult for you to part with your money? Statistics show that a minority of Christians tithe ten percent of their income. God's own people hinder His hand from moving supernaturally on their behalf. Are circumstances dictating your obedience or disobedience to God in financial matters?

Maybe you hold back your tithe because you feel the church is manipulating your money out of you. Maybe they are. You must still obey God! You are held accountable for obedience with your tithe regardless of what manipulation occurred. It is up to you where you sow your offerings but the tithe belongs in the house God placed you in. Are you in the right house?

Leaders in the church who misuse funds must answer to God for stewardship of the money that comes into the house of God. Let God deal with them. You do your part in what God asked of you. Don't miss out on God's blessings because someone else may be disobeying God.

Do you withhold your tithe because you think the church doesn't need your money? Do not be deceived! It requires money to spread the gospel to the nations. The pastor, his staff and their families need to eat and buy clothing just as you do. Electricity, water and heat are not free for church buildings. Mission trips to foreign countries are not expense free. It takes money to put Bibles in people's hands. It requires money to help the poor and underprivileged. It costs money to run the ministry God called you to. Are you doing your part in funding the gospel of Jesus Christ, the One who died for you?

## ANOTHER LESSON IN GIVING –
## CHIPPING OFF A STONY HEART

Obedience to tithing and giving offerings was only a beginning for me. It merely scratched the surface of a selfish, ungiving heart. On the outside the appearance of generosity existed but on the inside God still had a major work to do in my heart. God sees and knows our hearts (1 Samuel 16:7).

God revealed the stronghold material things had on me. How painful it was to see the condition of my heart as God held a spiritual mirror in front of me. I saw the reflection of a stony, selfish heart. Another area of weakness exposed itself. Change was on the horizon once again.

Shortly after purchasing a beautiful oak dining room table and chairs, my husband and I discovered our active family needed something more practical. Late Friday afternoon I made arrangements to place an ad in the newspaper so we could sell our set and purchase one better suited to our needs. Confident we would find success in snapping up a quick sale, we expected the phone to begin ringing on Monday morning.

While waiting for service to start on Sunday morning, I scanned the church bulletin. A notice jumped out highlighting a Russian ministry in need of household furniture. I instantly sensed a strong impression in my spirit. *Give your dining set to this ministry.*

*You want me to give what*? I almost blurted out. I quickly pushed the thought out of my mind, silently trying to convince myself that my imagination was working overtime. Unconvinced, I subtly turned around to see who had spoken but the seats were empty.

*God surely wouldn't tell me to give it away, would He?* I thought.

*After all, He knows we need the money from the sale of our table in order to buy another table. He knows we just placed an ad in the newspaper, doesn't He?*

After discussing the dilemma with Tom, I quickly realized God wanted to deal with me, as Tom supported giving or selling the furniture. He left the decision to me.

I wrestled in my spirit for the remainder of the day. Unable to sleep, I continued wrestling throughout the night. The oak furniture stuck in my mind as a spiritual battle raged in my heart. Desperate to find peace, I considered compromising. *I'll donate the set "if" it doesn't sell within one week.* The suggestion of compromise made me feel even worse.

Determined to press through my restlessness, spiritual fog gradually lifted as obedience to God became clear. When morning dawned, I quickly surrendered to God's leading. Still in my bathrobe, I shuffled through papers to find the church bulletin. Like a child anxiously waiting to divulge a secret, I could hardly wait to make the call.

"Does your ministry possibly need a dining room set?" I asked. Without hesitation, the woman gratefully took me up on my offer.

Compassion stirred in my heart when she told me about a Russian family of nine who had arrived in the states with nothing but the clothes on their back. "They have no furniture. Not even a table to eat on." Peace rose in my spirit as I realized it *was* God's voice I heard.

"We won't be able to give you a receipt for tax purposes," she added. "I'll understand if you want to change your mind."

"I don't need a receipt," I said. No longer blind, I knew a tax write off was irrelevant to my obedience.

After making arrangements to pick up the furniture, she added, "Thank you for obeying what God asked you to do."

*How did she know?* I thought. I had not shared my story with her, as I was too ashamed to expose my spiritual struggle of obedience.

Hanging up the phone, "Whatever you did for one of the least of these brothers of mine, you did for me" (Matthew 25:40), and "God loves a cheerful giver" (2 Corinthians 9:7) surfaced in my spirit. Overwhelmed by God's grace, tears of repentance fell to the floor.

I wept as my heart of stone was divinely transformed in a heavenly moment.

The Russian man arrived at our home with an interpreter the next day. His eyes watered when I led him to his new furniture. Emotionally charged foreign words poured from his mouth while he wiped his wet cheeks.

"He says he's never received anything so nice; he's never owned anything so nice. He's thankful," the interpreter explained.

"Thank you, thank you, thank you," he choked out as they loaded his gift into the back of his rusty truck and slowly drove away. I watched them disappear around the corner as I pondered the overflowing heart of gratitude I had witnessed.

The following week, the Russian ministry leader approached me with a beaming smile. "The family you donated your furniture to is known in Russia for their generous hearts," she said. "Every time we visit Russia, we hear testimonies of their sacrificial giving. Although they had little, they willingly gave of what they have." Then she divulged, "This family prayed and asked God for the furniture they needed. They trusted God to provide."

As calls started coming in from people responding to our newspaper ad, I joyfully explained, "I'm sorry, the furniture is already gone." I smiled, confident God's furniture was exactly where He intended it to be. I was just a tool He used to get it there.

What a tremendous blessing! Joy radiates from a giving heart. It is much more blessed to give than to receive. (Acts 20:35) It truly is! Giving is a privilege.

## EXAMINE YOUR MOTIVES FOR GIVING

When you feel led to give, examine your motives. Do you give to get praise from man? Do you give to be acknowledged by man? Are you offended because someone did not thank you for your giving? Check your motives. Did you do it for God or for man? Do you really want to keep your motives in check? Give anonymously.

Matthew 6:2-4 tells us how to give: "So when you give to the needy, do not announce it with trumpets, as the hypocrites do in the synagogues and on the streets, to be honored by men. I tell you the truth, they have received their reward in full. But when you give to the needy, do not let your left hand know what your right hand is doing, so that your giving may be in secret. Then your Father, who sees what is done in secret, will reward you." The end result of our giving should be that God is given the glory and the thanksgiving. Bringing glory to God should be the motive behind *all* of our giving.

## SOWING AND REAPING – A SPIRITUAL LAW

God established some key spiritual laws that will be in place as long as the earth endures. Just as cold and heat, summer and winter, and day and night will never cease, the law of seedtime and harvest will never cease (Genesis 8:22). The law of sowing and reaping has been established by God and will not change. You reap what you sow.

As you sow seed through giving, God continues to give you more seed! God supplies seed to the faithful sower and also supplies and increases his store of seed (2 Corinthians 9:10). Luke 6:38 explains what happens when you give: "Give and it will be given to you. A good measure, pressed down, shaken together and running over, will be poured into your lap. For with the measure you use, it will be measured to you." You will never run out of a supply of seed when you sow into the kingdom of God because God keeps filling you up. You cannot outgive God!

Be generous in your giving and you yourself will prosper. You always reap what you sow. Sow big, reap big. Sow small, reap small. It is a spiritual law and God's promise (2 Corinthians 9:6). Do not forget a key to giving: give with a cheerful heart!

## WAS THAT YOU, GOD?

God may ask you to give a precious or sentimental material possession. He may ask you to give something that is not easy for you to part with. Does that material thing have a hold on you? Do what God asks of you. You'll be blessed in the process.

Scurrying into church one morning, I found the door to the Sunday School Class already shut tight. *Oh no, I'm late.* My habitual chatting before class once again left me behind schedule. Cracking the door open, I crept in quietly and slid into the seat next to Tom.

Just as I got papers settled and my Bible opened, the Lord's voice startled me. *I want you to give your fur coat to Kim.* The teacher continued with class, but my mind quickly drifted off to my coat. I had saved money for several years before accumulating enough to buy a fur coat. I wore the stunning blue fox fur only on special occasions throughout the chilly winter months. The remainder of the year it rested safely in a temperature controlled environment. I hadn't thought about my fur for several months as it had been tucked away in storage for the season.

Although the heavenly instruction came unexpectedly, I recognized the familiar voice of the Holy Spirit. It would not be my own idea to give my coat away as it was the only elegant coat I had ever owned. I knew Satan had not planted the idea in my mind either, as it is not his practice to prompt God's people to bless others.

Returning home from church, I told Tom that God prompted me to bless Kim with my coat. Tom's response left me awestruck. "Hun, you won't believe this," he said. "Before you came into Sunday School class, Kim told the class that while she was in Chicago the previous week, she tried on someone's fur coat. She said that after lavishing in the coat, she and her husband agreed in prayer for a fur coat of her own."

Tom mused, "As I listened to Kim's story, I thought to myself, *Therese is going to give her the blue fox fur coat.* I guess that wasn't my own thought." Kim was the woman the Lord told me to give my coat to!

That was all the confirmation I needed. With no understanding of why God wanted me to give Kim my coat, I welcomed the opportunity to be used by God.

After taking the fur out of storage I brought it to a furrier to be cleaned, as I wanted Kim's gift to be fresh and crisp. Before the coat was ready for pick up, I received news of my mother's sudden death. I dashed out of town the next day, unable to deliver Kim's coat as planned.

Returning home after the funeral, the reality of my mother's death hit me, leaving me grief ridden and emotionally numb. God's direction regarding my coat stayed in the forefront of my thoughts though, so I pressed through the fog of sorrow to obey God.

Kim answered the phone when I called. "Kim? I have a gift for you. Could you stop by to pick it up?"

"A gift for me? Sure! We'll stop by after work."

When Kim and her husband arrived, her inquisitive eyes revealed the questions in her mind. After briefly filling them in about my mother's funeral, I got to the point. "Wait here. I have something for you." I dashed upstairs and returned with the coat in hand. Flooded with emotion, I came from behind and slid the coat on Kim. "This is your coat."

Kim wrapped her arms around herself, feeling the soft fur as tears streamed down her flushed cheeks. She tried to speak but hesitated.

"I received a prophetic word last year. God said He was going to give me a special gift." She choked as she continued. "He said He was going to give me this gift just because He loves me and wants to bless my obedience to Him. He said I'd know when I received His gift. *This is my gift! This* is the gift God was talking about!"

Kim's husband smiled in disbelief. "When we were in Chicago, we agreed in prayer for a fur coat. We told God we'd hold out for a particular fur. *A blue fox fur.*"

My grief suddenly dissipated. The refreshing wind of exuberant joy blew through the house. Stepping through the sorrow of my mother's death, I sensed Mom was standing right next to God, smiling down on the emotionally charged scene taking place in my home.

My coat warmed its new owner as she left hand in hand with her grinning husband. As I watched the couple disappear down the driveway, a blanket of healing love fell from heaven. "He who refreshes others will himself be refreshed" (Proverbs 11:25).

Why did God ask me to give her my coat? I didn't have time to figure out God's reasoning. I was too busy bouncing with joy because I realized material things no longer had a hold on me. I had the privilege of giving with a cheerful heart! Don't miss an opportunity to give as the Lord leads.

## THE MASTER WILL TEACH YOU – ARE YOU WILLING?

Is giving a struggle for you? Ask God to change your heart. If you are willing, He will transform you. God, out of His abundant mercy and love, will change your heart through divine methods. Submit yourself to the Master and allow Him to teach you how to give with a willing and cheerful heart.

God gave what was most precious to Him – His Son Jesus. He made the ultimate sacrifice to give His best. He sacrificed Himself knowing many would reject Him. He selflessly gave of Himself knowing many would never acknowledge or appreciate His gift. He gave out of a heart of unconditional love and as a result we have eternal life. How can we deny Him?

# CHAPTER 8
# Christianity Is Not A Popularity Contest

## FOLLOWING CHRIST IS NOT POPULAR
## IN THE WORLD'S EYES

You're born again! You're a new creation in Christ Jesus. Halleluia!

Life as a Christian will be bliss and trouble free, right? *Wrong*. Increasing wickedness in the world creates continuous challenges for the committed Christian.

How do you live *in* a world full of sin yet not be *of* the world full of sin? How do you demonstrate evidence that you are a follower of Christ instead of appearing so carnal that one cannot tell the difference between you and a heathen?

God provided a perfect instruction manual to direct your earthly venture on the path leading to life. The narrow path to eternal life is the unpopular route that many do not choose (Matthew 7:14). Many people unknowingly follow the popular path, not realizing it leads to certain destruction. To live for Jesus Christ and according to His Word, you must face the reality that Christianity is not a popularity contest.

## CHRISTIANS WILL BE PERSECUTED

When you became a follower of Jesus Christ, it was likely not long before you realized the unbelieving world is not always excited about hearing the good news of the gospel. Sharing the message of the cross can bring an undesirable response from some unbelievers. You may be coldly rejected because of your love and commitment to the Lord Jesus.

As you take a stand for righteousness and choose God's way instead of the world's way, you may be labeled as odd and called insulting and unpopular names. You are odd according to the world's standards. Jesus told His disciples, "If the world hates you, keep in mind that it hated me first. If you belonged to the world, it would love you as its own. As it is, you do not belong to the world, but I have chosen you out of the world. That is why the world hates you" (John 15:18-19). You are a foreigner in a strange land.

Jesus warned of coming persecution to everyone who wants to live a godly life in Him (2 Timothy 3:12). People may laugh at your "goodie-two-shoes" Christian lifestyle. You may be a target for ridicule and gossip. Many followers of Christ have shed blood or lost their lives because of their Christian faith. While Jesus was on earth healing and delivering people from oppression of the devil, he was rejected and persecuted by man. Jesus did not cave in when He was persecuted for doing His Father's will, but instead pressed on all the way to the cross. Press on!

Children are sometimes persecuted for following the training and instruction of the Lord. Mounting worldly pressure entices children to follow the popular crowd. "But Mom, everyone else is doing it" echoes in parents' ears.

Can you withstand the pressure from the majority who set their moral gauge by the world's standards? What have you allowed in your children's lives because you did not want to risk them being unpopular among their peers? Have you compromised God's Word?

Parents must instill a strong confidence in their children based on knowing they are sons and daughters of God, forgiven, and loved by Him. If a child grasps the revelation of his identity in Christ, the approval or disapproval of his peers will have little effect on him. He will value himself because God values him, not because other people say he is valuable or worthless.

It is a powerful testimony when a young person chooses not to take part in activities that dishonor God, yet demonstrates love to those who do. He loves them without being like them. Often the others eventually wonder why the Christian kids are genuinely content with a "clean" life. Finding only heartache in a destructive lifestyle, they search for hope. Children can be a powerful witness to other young people who desperately search for answers.

## STANDING FIRM FOR YOUR CHILDREN

Christian parents are often accused of controlling their children by influencing their environments and monitoring their activities. "Let kids make their own choices," parents are advised. Accepting worldly counsel leaves many parents oblivious of the fact that their children are sexually active, testing out lethal drugs or viewing pornography on the Internet. Destructive activities and addictions are developing right under their own roof, yet parents don't have the slightest inkling that anything is amiss until life-changing damage is done.

Regardless of what the world dictates, it's you, parents, not your neighbors, that will stand before God to give account of how you raised your children. God clearly gave parents the responsibility to raise children up in the training and instruction of the Lord (Ephesians 6:4). Those questioning your choices will not be held accountable for your children – you will.

When children become adults, they will make their own choices. You cannot control their choices after your job of parenting is done except through prayer, example and counsel. It is your responsibility, however, to train them according to God's ways while they are in your care. God's desire is clear: "Fix these words of mine in your hearts and minds; tie them as symbols on your hands and bind them on your foreheads. Teach them to your children, talking about them when you sit at home and when you walk along the road, when you lie down and when you get up" (Deuteronomy 11:18-19). Are the world's words or God's words engrained in your children? Stand firm for your children, parents. The seeds of righteousness you sow produce everlasting fruit.

## TOLERANCE AND COMPROMISE

The world belligerently shouts, "Accept anything and everything regardless of how immoral or destructive it is!" The world boasts of its twisted standards: "Of course abortion is acceptable, it's only a mass of tissue we're getting rid of, not a baby." "Practicing homosexuality is just an alternate lifestyle. After all, God created the homosexual." "If you're not happy with your spouse, get a divorce and find a new one." "If you aren't getting what you need at home, a little affair on the side won't hurt anybody." "Lying isn't that big of a deal. What will a little white lie hurt?" The world's voice is loud and obnoxious. The world's mouth is full of lies that lure people into a snare of destruction. If you do not tolerate the world's lies, it wags its accusing finger of shame and says, "Intolerant!"

The world strives to drill tolerance into our minds. The dreaded name "intolerant" is pinned on those who stand for the truth of God's Word. "No," the world tells us, "there is no one truth." Josh McDowell writes, "This new tolerance considers every individual's beliefs, values, lifestyles and truth claims as equally valid. So not only does everyone have an equal right to his beliefs, but all beliefs are equal. The new tolerance goes beyond respecting a person's rights; it demands praise and endorsement of that person's beliefs, values and lifestyles." He adds, "Because the new tolerance declares all beliefs equally valid, Christians face increasing pressure to be silent about their convictions – in school, at work, in the public square – because to speak out will be seen as an intolerant judgement of other's beliefs and lifestyles."[1] The devil is fighting diligently to silence Christians. Has he silenced you?

## LOVE THE SINNER, NOT THE SIN

If the Bible is our guide, then winking approvingly at sin cannot be our practice. God certainly does not approve of sin. Praise God, He forgives the sinner, yet instructs him to sin no more. God did not teach anyone to continue in sin, to embrace a lifestyle of sin or to wink at sin. It is God's desire for us to embrace all people, but not necessarily to embrace their beliefs.

Jesus forgave the woman shamefully caught in the act of adultery. He did not condemn her, but instead willingly forgave her. Did Jesus grant the woman a license to continue her lifestyle of sexual immorality? No! He lovingly told her to leave her life of sin (John 8:11). It requires love not only to lead people out of a life of sin, but to lead them into a life of abundance in Christ as well.

God willingly forgives the repentant sinner who desires to turn from sin. We should be forever grateful that God is slow to anger and patient in waiting for us to repent from our wicked ways. Those refusing to turn from sin, however, eventually suffer the wrath of

God. Although God is a God of love, He must judge sin.

Do not be deceived. Sin is sin. God came to save the sinner but did not make a way for him to continue in his sin. God cannot be mocked. A man reaps what he sows (Galatians 6:7-8). Sin leads to sure destruction.

Are we to approve of sin and rebellion against God? No! But in our disapproval, let us not forget to hate the sin, yet love the sinner. The unbelieving world does not understand this concept because its moral compass is off. A follower of Christ must learn to love the sinner without approving of his sin.

Josh McDowell shares tremendous wisdom in addressing the sin of tolerance with love: "Tolerance says, 'You must approve of what I do.' Love responds, 'I must do something harder; I will love you, even when your behavior offends me.' Tolerance says, 'You must agree with me.' Love responds, 'I must do something harder; I will tell you the truth because I am convinced 'the truth will set you free.' Tolerance says, 'You must allow me to have my way.' Love responds, 'I must do something harder; I will plead with you to follow the right way, because I believe you are worth the risk.' Tolerance seeks to be inoffensive; love takes risks. Tolerance glorifies division; love seeks unity. Tolerance costs nothing; love costs everything."[2] Love conquers the destructive and deceptive teaching of tolerance.

When you take a stand for righteousness, you may be labeled intolerant or be ridiculed for refusing to embrace the sin that the world pressures you to tolerate. God does not tolerate sin but instead responds to the sinner in love. We must do the same.

## STANDING ALONE

At one time or another you will experience situations requiring you to stand for what you believe. Get off the fence of lukewarm Christianity and become committed to the uncompromised gospel of Jesus Christ!

You may be alone in choosing not to participate in an activity that you know displeases God. Maybe you're the only one in the crowd foregoing an inappropriate movie. Are you going to stand for what God desires or are you going to cave in because you cannot endure potential persecution?

God's ways are not the world's ways. James 4:4 tells us we must make a choice: "You adulterous people, don't you know that friendship with the world is hatred toward God? Anyone who chooses to be a friend of the world becomes an enemy of God." Being a friend of the world through compromise is not the answer.

A committed follower of Christ must be willing to stand alone. It is easy to follow what the world dictates as acceptable but it takes backbone to stand for what you believe. Many well-meaning Christians silently hide out in fear of persecution or ridicule. Are you using God's moral compass or the world's moral compass?

When you refuse the world's standards and follow the uncompromised gospel of Jesus Christ, some people will not like it. "Well," they may mutter in disgust. "Isn't he just pathetically self-righteous." "Hmm," they may sneer with gritted teeth, "I'll just bet those religious freaks think they're better than we are because they go to church and we don't."

Even other Christians may encourage compromise as they voice their disapproval. "What?" they may sputter in disbelief. "You won't come to the movie with us? For goodness sake, aren't you going a bit over board? Can't you just close your eyes during the scenes that bother you?" Don't be offended; continue to live for Christ with joy and let your light shine.

Along with the benefits of computer technology and media advancements comes opportunity for immorality to find its way into our homes. Although most people wouldn't dream of inviting strangers into their living room to disrobe, participate in sexual immorality, use foul language or practice violence, they often don't realize these things flow into their homes through their television or VCR. Godly wisdom will lead us to guard our homes from evil influences.

A submitted child of God does not make choices based on the world's standards or the world's approval. A believer seeking God's best makes choices based on God's Word. Are you conforming to the world's standards through popular opinion or striving to conform to the image of Jesus Christ? Paul tells us, "Do not be conformed to this world, but be transformed by the renewing of your mind, that you may prove what is that good and acceptable and perfect will of God" (Romans 12:2, NKJV). Do you resemble the world or do you resemble Jesus?

Do you want to win man's approval or God's approval? If you desire man's approval, you will never discover true victory in Christ. Life in Jesus Christ is not a popularity contest. Jesus was famous throughout His ministry, but was certainly not popular. If you are looking to obtain worldly approval on your Christian journey, you will be disappointed. If you seek God's approval, however, you are headed for sure victory in this life and into eternity.

## DOESN'T EVERYBODY WANT TO GET SAVED?

I remember feeling as if I would burst with joy after committing my life to serving God. As my spiritual eyes were opened, the revelation settled in my heart that I was forgiven of all sin and would spend eternity with Jesus. I felt so clean – so new. Hope for a future sprung forth from my soul.

I willingly told others about Jesus, fully confident they would also want to accept Him as Lord and Savior. My bubble of joy burst as I quickly learned that not everyone wanted the gift Jesus offered. In fact, few wanted to even hear about Him.

"That religious nonsense may be for you, but it's not for me," laughed some. "I'm a good person, I don't need that Jesus stuff," others claimed, ignorantly putting their confidence in their good works for salvation. I grieved as I realized many put their trust in infant baptism. "I was baptized as a baby, my eternity is already taken care of." Some, not realizing they may face an untimely death, declared, "I'm still young, I've got lots of time before I have to worry about where I stand with God." I thought of the man in the parable of the rich fool (Luke 12:16-21) who made a similar statement before God said, "You fool! This very night your life will be demanded from you." *Dear God!* I cried. *They don't understand.*

Deflated by the rejection I received, I became deeply concerned about the unsaved. Some people did not understand that Jesus was the only way to eternal life (John 14:6). They did not understand the cross of Calvary. I desperately wanted them to embrace the truth of salvation and feared many of the people I loved would not spend eternity in heaven. "What am I going to do, Lord?" I asked God in flawed desperation. "What am *I* going to do?"

You must come to the realization, as I did, that you may not be the one who effectively ministers the message of the cross to your loved ones. You may plant seeds or water seeds of truth, yet not be given the opportunity to pray with them to receive Christ.

God uses many methods of revealing the truth to those who do not know Him. Share the hope you have in Jesus as led by the Holy Spirit, but let God minister to people's hearts in the way He chooses. Put your plan aside and allow God to work out His plan.

## ACTIONS SPEAK LOUDER THAN WORDS

If unbelieving loved ones resist the truth of the gospel, don't lose hope. Your life and your actions will continue to speak much louder than any words you could possibly share. Your demonstration of faith in God and His Word is a constant and powerful witness to unbelievers around you. Peter tells us to "live such good lives among the pagans that, though they accuse you of doing wrong, they may see your good deeds and glorify God on the day he visits us" (1 Peter 2:12). You may not realize it, but people continually observe your life, listen carefully to your words and watch your actions. Let your light shine!

Although *you* know you are a new creation in Christ Jesus, it may take time for others to see the transformation taking place in you, especially if your life as an unbeliever included ungodly activities as mine did. Your testimony of faith in Jesus may be initially rejected because of the things you practiced prior to being saved. "She'll get over this 'Jesus thing' in time," they may snicker in disbelief. "It's just a phase she's going through. Before long she'll be right back to her old life." As a child of the King of Kings, stand strong with your head held high. Press on and finish the race!

Paul, who was mightily used of God and who wrote a good portion of the New Testament, called himself the "chief of sinners." Before his conversion, when he was called Saul, he watched approvingly as the Apostle Stephen was stoned to death. Prior to putting his faith in Jesus, he was known for persecution and abuse of Christians. Everything changed when God, through His grace and mercy, showed up on the scene and grabbed hold of Paul's heart.

Although God radically changed Paul, it took time for others to believe he had been changed. They could not forget Paul's past: "'Isn't he the man who raised havoc in Jerusalem among those who call on this name? And hasn't he come here to take them as prisoners to the chief priests?' Yet Saul grew more and more powerful and baffled the Jews living in Damascus by proving that Jesus is the Christ" (Acts 9:21-22).

Paul baffled the Jews. You too will baffle people when they witness God's transforming power operating in your life. If God got a hold of your heart as He got a hold of Paul's heart, you'll never be the same again. Be patient and keep your eyes focussed on your relationship with God. Your demonstration of the attributes of Christ impacts those around you and testifies of the One who dwells within you. You are a walking testimony!

## IMPACT YOUR LOVED ONES THROUGH PRAYER

Although loved ones may not be receptive to the truth of salvation from you directly, you can bring God's supernatural work into their lives through prayer. Moishe Rosen of Jews for Jesus said it best: "When you can't talk to your friends about God you can always talk to God about your friends."[3]

Pray diligently for the salvation of unbelievers by asking God to open the eyes of their hearts. Ask God to send people across their path to share the truth of the Word of God, as they need to hear the truth in order to respond to the truth. Your loved ones may be more receptive to receiving God's Word from someone other than you. The Lord tells us to ask Him to send workers across into the harvest field (Luke 10:2). Ask Him! He is faithful.

God sent several people to me who shared the hope they had in Jesus years before I chose to follow Him. I wasn't interested in hearing the message of the cross at that time. "Oh no, here comes one of those 'holy rollers' again," I scoffed. "What an utterly boring life those 'born again' people must have," I laughed arrogantly, not even knowing what "born again" meant.

Little did I realize that the born again holy rollers I laughed at possessed exactly what I needed. Regardless of how desperately those servants of God wanted me to give my life to Christ, it couldn't happen until I understood and received the truth. The veil had to be lifted from my spiritual eyes before I could surrender my life to God. *Someone, somewhere was praying for me.*

## GOD'S WORD WILL NOT RETURN VOID

After I accepted Jesus as Lord, the words of the faithful people who shared the Good News of the gospel came back to my remembrance. With newly opened spiritual eyes, I understood what they tried to tell me about Jesus. God's Word did not and will not return void. Every Word spoken from the mouth of God is pregnant with purpose. His Word never returns empty, but accomplishes the purpose God sent it to accomplish (Isaiah 55:11).

Keep hope alive for your loved ones. God's plan and timing are perfect. I thank God that someone was praying for my salvation while I was floundering around in the world. Someone prayed for my eyes to be opened. It is God's will that none should perish but that *all* would come to know Him (2 Peter 3:9).

## ARE YOU GETTING IN GOD'S WAY?

Sometimes we get in God's way by fretting and interfering with His plan in other people's lives. We often muck up His plan by forcing our own plan into action. By releasing our loved ones into God's hands, we enable Him to do His work in His time and in His way.

God loves unbelievers and wants them to know Him personally even more than we do. As we pray, obey God and share the gospel, God is at work. We cannot save any human being nor can we draw him into the kingdom of God. That's God's job (John 6:44).

Our Counselor, the precious Holy Spirit, convicts the world of sin. It is not our role to convict unbelievers of their sin. Even the Holy Spirit brings conviction to the unbeliever of one sin and one sin alone – for not believing in Jesus Christ (John 16:7-11). Let the Holy Spirit do His work.

Believers often make the mistake of trying to play the Holy Spirit's role. God never intended for us to fill that role. Being a witness for Jesus Christ and preaching the gospel is our role, not judging those outside the church (1 Corinthians 5:12).

## CONTINUE TO LOVE UNBELIEVERS

If your loved ones reject the truth of the gospel, continue to love them unconditionally. Keep an eye on your attitude toward those who reject you and make sure it reflects the example Jesus gave us. Your attitude should be the same as that of Christ Jesus (Philippians 2:5).

Jesus loved those who rejected Him. While suffering on the cross, He asked His Father to forgive those who sent Him there and those who hated Him. How is your attitude toward those who reject you? Choose to love them regardless of the rejection or ridicule you receive. Let your unconditional love minister to them.

Avoid condemning unbelievers who make choices you disagree with. Do you remember life before you were born again? Do you recall the poor choices you may have made? Do you remember the activities you participated in? You too were blinded and could not see. Love those who are in darkness. Love those who persecute you. Your demonstration of nonjudgmental and unconditional love can draw them to the kingdom.

## UNBELIEVERS ARE SPIRITUALLY BLIND

Christians often get frustrated when unbelievers do not willingly receive the truth of the gospel. Before understanding salvation and accepting Christ as Savior, people are spiritually blind. Have you ever shuffled around with a blindfold on? Do you remember the pin-the-tail-on-the-donkey game? Stumbling and bumping into walls are certain when you cannot see. You were unable to see clearly until the blindfold was removed.

Likewise, in the spiritual realm unbelievers cannot understand or accept the things of God because their eyes are blinded. To the unbeliever, the truths that come from the Spirit of God are foolishness. He needs the Spirit of God in order to understand the things of God because they are spiritually discerned (1 Corinthians 2:14). Although it is God's will for the unbeliever to know Him, he cannot see the truth until the spiritual blinders are removed.

Don't take it personally when someone rejects the truth you share. He may be blind! Are you frustrated with a blind man because he cannot see? Because Satan blinds the minds of unbelievers, they cannot see the truth of the gospel (2 Corinthians 4:4). The good news is that God can open blind eyes. Keep praying! The blinders covering their spiritual eyes will be removed at the perfect time. Once they understand the truth they will have to make a choice. Everybody eventually must make a choice.

As you are transformed into the image of Jesus Christ, your light burns brightly with a loud testimony. Even though blind eyes may not see the truth of the spoken Word, your life is a living testimony to those around you. Let your light shine before men (Matthew 5:16). Continue to let the glory of the Lord shine through you! Changed lives draw the world to Jesus.

## RELATIONSHIPS CHANGE
## WHEN YOU COME INTO THE KINGDOM

Some who knew you before you came to the Lord may prefer to have the old you back and may not share the joy of your new life in Christ. They likely do not understand the change in you. You cannot control what others' reactions are to your choice to live for Jesus. Do not let the negative reaction pull you down or slow your pace in the race.

When you surrender your life to Jesus, relationships may change. As God's Word renews your mind and is applied to your life, destructive behavior gradually falls away. In the process, relationships associated with the destructive behavior can fall away as well. It's a natural process. When relationships change or become distant, it can feel as emotionally draining as mourning a death. The loss rarely is without pain.

New life in Christ impacts close relationships. The presence of God penetrates *every* aspect of your life. As God transforms you, your new identity will become obvious to those around you. Your loved ones may or may not accept your faith in Christ. You may lead some into the kingdom of God, yet be persecuted and ridiculed by others. Regardless of the opinions or acceptance of those around you, you are now accountable to God.

God wants to be first in your life, above your most cherished relationships (Deuteronomy 5:7). Is God first in your life? He wants to be above your money, above your material possessions, and above your relationships. Is God taking second place to a relationship or is He above all? Has a relationship become a god to you? Do your relationships cause you to shrink back from your commitment to serving God, or do they encourage growth on your Christian journey?

## LOVE THE UNBELIEVER,
## BUT DO NOT BE YOKED WITH HIM

If someone rejects you and the God you serve, don't make the mistake of forcing a relationship to continue as it was before you knew God. Instead of your good character rubbing off on them, their bad character can rub off on you if you insist on continuing a close relationship. Bad company corrupts good character (1 Corinthians 15:33). Because you are a new creature in Christ (2 Corinthians 5:17), your relationship cannot and will not be the same as it was in the past. The old you is gone.

Be aware of the relationships you embrace. Close intimate relationships with unbelievers are no longer possible for you. This does not mean you are superior, nor does it indicate you should shut the unbeliever out of your life. How will we bring in a harvest of souls if we shut unbelievers out of our lives? We need to reach them!

A follower of Christ lives by a different belief system than an unbeliever, however, and the two cannot be in harmony when they are bound together in business, marriage, or close personal relationship. The Apostle Paul warns us, "Do not be yoked together with unbelievers. For what do righteousness and wickedness have in common? Or what fellowship can light have with darkness? What harmony is there between Christ and Belial? What does a believer have in common with an unbeliever?" (2 Corinthians 6:14-15). Forcing a close relationship to continue with an unbeliever invites trouble. The two cannot be in harmony.

Although our children are several years away from marriage, they know of God's desire for them to marry a believer. Even dating an unbeliever can lead to difficulties as the potential exists for developing romantic feelings and eventually pondering marriage. Marrying an unbeliever with hopes that he or she will eventually surrender to the Lordship of Jesus is not God's best either.

Extreme potential problems lurk when a believer becomes yoked in marriage to an unbeliever. This is *not* to say a believing spouse should abandon or divorce an unbelieving spouse, as Scripture tells us otherwise (1 Corinthians 7:13). Whether in marriage, or even a business venture, or close intimate friendship, to intentionally yoke oneself with an unbeliever can bring much unnecessary heartache.

Use godly wisdom in choosing and cultivating intimate relationships as your life is influenced and impacted by those closest to you. Are your friends building you up and encouraging you in godly pursuits or tearing you and others around you down? Are your friends exhorting others or gossiping and backbiting? Do they practice destructive activities or choose activities that honor God? Are they speaking faith or defeat into your life? Are they keeping records of others' wrongs or walking in love? Who has a voice in your life? Who influences you?

In the process of conforming to the image of Jesus Christ, some relationships that are harmful to your life in Christ may end or become distant. Praise God though, new God-ordained friendships begin to blossom. A friendship in the Lord is a gift from God. Ask God to establish your inner circle of friends for you. Commit your relationships to the Lord and He will bring you His best.

## ACKNOWLEDGING LOVE FOR CHRIST IN AN UNGODLY WORLD

As sin increases, the world's ways become increasingly immoral and ungodly. Will you continue to make your love for Jesus known to the world, or hide it because you fear persecution? Are you afraid to acknowledge your Lord and Savior before man? Are you ashamed to give the Lord praise with your lips in the presence of others? Do you join hands in prayer before meals at home yet avoid blessing your food in a restaurant? Are you a closet Christian? Why are you ashamed? If you acknowledge Jesus before men, Jesus will also acknowledge you before God but if you disown Jesus before men, you will be disowned before God (Matthew 10:32-33).

Multitudes of people are headed for hell. They need your testimony! They need to hear the truth of the gospel of Jesus Christ. The world needs to see a demonstration of God's teachings. Unless you are willing to be a witness for Christ, how will they ever know God's plan?

Are you willing to confess your love for Jesus before man? Praying for the salvation of unbelievers is critical, but you must be prepared to share the truth of God's Word when the door is opened. Faith cannot come until God's Word comes forth (Romans 10:17). You must be willing to open your mouth.

Ask God to open doors of opportunity for you to share the gospel. Be sensitive to recognize when the door is open, as it is often when you least expect it. Forcing the gospel on unbelievers, threatening them with hell's flames or putting your own plan into action will rarely produce the result you desire. Let God schedule the divine appointments and be prepared to share the testimony of your hope (1 Peter 3:15).

Shortly after Tom made the decision to follow Christ, he spoke heart-piercing words. He confessed, "I wish someone had told me about salvation through Jesus earlier in my life. I wish I had heard the truth sooner." How many others are searching for the truth and waiting for someone to open their mouth? Multitudes are searching for the hope only Jesus can give.

## ARE YOU JUDGING WHO IS WORTHY TO HEAR THE GOSPEL?

Why do believers hesitate to share the gospel of Jesus Christ with the unsaved? Christians often unconsciously prejudge who will and who will not receive the message of the cross. By judging someone's appearance or stature, we determine whether or not he will accept us and the message we carry about Jesus.

Do we have a preconceived notion that the wealthy won't listen? We may think, *That man looks like he has everything. He seems so happy and prosperous. I bet he won't think he needs a Savior.* Before I knew Christ, I appeared to enjoy the perfect life. A big smile appeared on my face while I was sinking in spiritual quicksand. Appearances are deceiving.

Do we assume people with a rough appearance will mock and reject us if we share our testimony with them? Are we waiting for assurance of personal acceptance before we will open our mouth?

God once gave me a sobering vision of an unbeliever I had hesitated to share the gospel with. Tormented in the eternal flames of hell, he looked up at me enjoying the blessings of heaven and pleaded, "Why didn't you tell me about Jesus? You knew the truth and you didn't tell me... Why didn't you tell me?" Oh, the heartache I felt at the thought of it! That vision was seared into my conscience and prompts me to open my mouth when God brings a lost soul my way.

The rich, the poor, the homely and the beautiful all need Jesus! *Every* person on earth needs to hear about Jesus. We must be willing to open our mouth when God gives us the opportunity. We possess the ability to impact the eternity of a lost soul. The harvest is ripe; let your testimony bring in a harvest!

One summer I packed up my three children and headed to a local amusement park for a day of roller coasters, food and fun. We arrived early in the morning and found only a handful of people filtering into the park. After filling the kids' fists with tickets, I sent them off to the rides and slid onto a bench to enjoy a relaxing break in the morning sun.

Ready to soak in a peaceful moment, I glanced across the park and spotted a man with long stringy hair and torn pants. The undeniable, still small voice of the Holy Spirit instantly rose up in my spirit. *I want you to share your testimony with that man.*

I silently grumbled to the Lord, *Now wait a minute, Lord, you must be kidding! Do you see him? I can't talk to him; he's too scary looking. Look at his hair, and those hippie glasses! Surely you couldn't possibly want me to share my testimony with him. He won't listen. I couldn't have heard you right, Lord!*

I continued my heavenly debate until I realized God was not going to change His mind. I drew in a deep breath as the tattered man sauntered across the park heading in my direction. Although there were hundreds of other empty seats available, he plopped down right next to me. Like a perfectly rehearsed scene, the Lord opened the conversation for me to share my testimony with my new friend, Tommy.

Tommy eagerly talked about the rock band he played in at a local bar. A look of surprise fell on his face when I told him that our church musicians had recently recorded a Christian CD. "I thought churches only sang hymns," he laughed, then continued to quiz me about the music.

Remembering my past church experiences, I identified with his stereotypical feelings. "I used to think the same thing about church too. Church was the last place I wanted to be back then." As we talked, the distinct smell of stale alcohol on Tommy's breath reminded me of my old lifestyle.

I divulged my past alcohol abuse and shared my search for hope through avenues leading to destruction and heartache. "I used to drink a lot, Tommy. I thought alcohol could fill the emptiness in my heart." My memory flooded with remembrance of past drinking days. "The emptiness was always there the next morning though."

Tommy's round wire-rimmed glasses slid down his nose, revealing eyes that reflected a beautiful man hidden under a hurting heart. He listened intently and nodded in agreement when I shared memories of drinking so much that I had no memory of driving home. His eyes watered when I recalled the guilt I felt over driving under the influence of alcohol with my baby in the back seat. "I risked my baby's life," I confessed. My past pain seemed strangely familiar to Tommy.

"One day I was introduced to Jesus and finally discovered the hope I searched for." I paused and smiled, being refreshed at my own testimony. "My life of destruction and hopelessness transformed into a life of abundance and hope through Jesus. That emptiness could only be filled with Jesus." Tommy subtly wiped his eyes, but continued to listen without taking his eyes off me.

"Do you know Jesus?" I asked Tommy. He glanced away briefly and then looked back into my eyes.

"We've talked," he said, pondering his own words.

His children interrupted us, begging their dad to stay longer but Tommy was quick to remind them of a bus that was only minutes away.

"Why don't you visit our church so you can hear some fellow musicians," I suggested. He took directions to the church and assured me he would try to make it to a service. After brief good byes, they hurried off to the bus stop.

Alone once again, I wondered why God arranged my unexpected meeting with Tommy. *Why did God ask me to share my story?*

I remembered that only hours before meeting Tommy, I asked God in prayer to use me for His glory. I petitioned God to bring a lost soul across my path that needed to hear about the love of Jesus. God had a divine purpose for my brief encounter with Tommy.

How thankful I was that God used me in spite of my hesitation and grumbling. I repented and humbly thanked God for allowing me to see Tommy through His eyes. Eyes of love.

I still pray for Tommy and sometimes glance back at the church entrance expecting him to walk through the door. The day may arrive when Tommy wakes up in a drunken stupor, ready to give up on life. Maybe the Holy Spirit will bring to his remembrance the lady at the park that found hope in Jesus. He may cry out to the heavens as I did long ago. Who knows? Maybe Tommy is talking to Jesus right now.

Christians frequently plead for an opportunity to be used by God. We ask God to bring people across our paths that need Jesus, yet when God brings them, are we willing to testify or are we only willing to accept the easy assignments that meet our own personal approval and comfort level?

I almost missed an opportunity to share the gospel of Jesus Christ with a lost soul because I prejudged his unwillingness to listen to me. My appointment with Tommy taught me that it is not up to me to judge who will listen when God asks me to speak. My responsibility is to obey God's direction, regardless of who He sends my way.

Do you prejudge who is and who is not worthy to receive the God's Word? Those you avoid could be the very ones crying out to God for the truth. They may be the ones on the verge of giving up on life. Before I accepted Christ, my outward appearance masked the emptiness that filled the inside. Appearances are deceiving and mean absolutely nothing. Let the Holy Spirit lead you and obey God when He opens the door for evangelism.

## STAND FIRM TO THE END

Although we live in a world that often mocks righteousness through Christ, you can choose to stand firm on the path illuminated with the truth of God's Word. God needs committed disciples set apart for His use. Friend in Christ, choose to live according to the *uncompromised* gospel of Jesus Christ. You are a walking testimony!

Jesus gave His life for you. Will you give your life for Him? You may be willing to die for Him... but are you willing to live for Him?

1   *Focus on the Family with Dr. James Dobson*, Monthly Magazine, August, 1999 edition, "Truth and Tolerance" article, by Josh McDowell, Page 6

2   Ibid. Page 7

3   *The Jews for Jesus Newsletter*, Volume 11:5760, July 2000, "Evangelism and Prayer" article, by David Brickner, Page 2

# CHAPTER 9
# Preparation For The Enemy

## GOD HAS AN ARMY

When you accepted Jesus as Lord and Savior, you were automatically enlisted in God's army. You are a soldier of the cross of Calvary. You are in a real battle with a real enemy.

An effective soldier knows his enemy. He studies the enemy's patterns, plans, and strategies. A soldier is equipped with powerful weaponry and is always prepared for surprise attacks. He respects the authority of his commanding officer and is committed to carrying out his orders without question.

As a member of God's army, you must know your enemy, Satan. You must be cognizant of his plans and strategies, be equipped with spiritual weapons, and, most of all, personally know and obey your commanding officer, God Himself.

## DO NOT BE IGNORANT – SATAN DOES EXIST

Satan's biggest scheme is convincing uninformed people that he doesn't really exist – that he is merely a make-believe figment of their imagination. He prides himself in being depicted as a harmless fictitious being with pointy horns who lives in hell with a pitchfork at his side.

The devil does not want to expose the truth that he freely roams the earth. He whispers words dripping with deception. *There's no such thing as hell… of course everyone goes to heaven regardless of the choices he makes… after all, a God of love surely wouldn't send anyone to hell, would he?*

To promote ignorance, Satan gleefully pours out and spreads lies to believers and unbelievers alike. People believing these lies are no threat to the enemy or his destructive mission. He is the father of lies. Jesus, speaking to the Pharisees said, "You belong to your father, the devil, and you want to carry out your father's desire. He was a murderer from the beginning, not holding to the truth, for there is no truth in him. When he lies, he speaks his native language, for he is a liar and the father of lies" (John 8:44).

God does not want you to be ignorant of the devil. Ignorance of Satan's tactics and schemes can result in severe consequences in a Christian's life. With no knowledge of God's instruction about dealing with Satan, you expose yourself to deception. The devil will wiggle his way into your life through any available open door; lack of knowledge is an avenue he always takes advantage of. Be on the lookout as the adversary walks about like a roaring lion, seeking whom he may devour (1 Peter 5:8).

## WHO IS SATAN?

Satan is your enemy and the enemy of God. With no compassion or sympathy for you or for anyone else, he sets venomous traps to take believers' focus off of God. A viscous deceiver, the evil one strives to prevent you from fulfilling your destiny in Christ. The destroyer orchestrates evil plans and schemes, utilizing his demonic power to implement attacks. His assignment is to destroy both the righteous and the unrighteous alike. You must equip yourself through knowledge of God's Word for dealing with Satan or risk being defeated in battle.

Satan is the god (little g) of this world (2 Corinthians 4:4). Does that surprise you? He is not lounging in the black depths of hell casually waiting for his followers to join him. He is here on earth, diligently seeking to destroy anything associated with God's kingdom and is willing to take advantage of any willing body to accomplish his goal. Striving to keep the minds of unbelievers in darkness where they will not know Jesus, Satan personally blinds their minds.

## EVIL IS FROM SATAN – NOT FROM GOD

People often wonder why evil saturates the earth, perplexed at why innocent people experience disaster. Blaming God for the evil occurring on the earth, they wonder how a God of love could allow such tragedy. God does not cause evil. Satan, the god of this world, authors evil.

When Adam sinned in the Garden of Eden by eating of the tree of knowledge of good and evil, he sold out to the devil. Because of Adam's disobedience, dominion of the earth was relinquished to Satan. Serious consequences followed Adam's misguided choice to believe the lies of the devil.

Satan, the father of lies, is on a mission running rampant across the earth to steal, kill and destroy and will continue accelerating his efforts until his time runs out. But praise God, we are not left helpless or hopeless during Satan's rampage on earth. God has a plan.

## SATAN IS A DEFEATED FOE

Because of Jesus and the blood He shed for the forgiveness of sin, we are heaven bound for an eternity with God. What a future to behold! The devil's time on earth is about to expire and his future is eternal doom in the lake of fire where he will be tormented day and night forever and ever (Revelation 20:10). Satan's future is grim.

Do not be deceived in thinking Satan has no power. If the devil were powerless, Jesus would not have instructed us to take authority over him. If Satan had no power, Jesus would not have had to come to destroy his demonic works. The devil does possess power to steal, to kill and to destroy (John 10:10). He is surely relentless.

Jesus came to earth to destroy the works of the devil (1 John 3:8) and made a way for us to overcome the works of the devil. Our Lord and Savior indeed conquered and destroyed the devil's work (Colossians 2:15). Halleluia! Jesus disarmed Satan at the cross of Calvary and made him a defeated foe! The authority Adam relinquished in the garden was bought back by Jesus!

Satan is a poor loser, and tries to occupy the victory seat even though he doesn't belong there. He is victorious in his own eyes only though. Just as a child uses his little hand to make huge shadow monsters on the wall, the enemy tries to make himself appear bigger than he really is. He has no rights or privileges in a Christian's life. He is a wimpy bully trying to exercise authority he does not possess.

Jesus conquered the devil at the cross and gave believers

authority to overcome any tactic or scheme he plans against them. You have authority to overcome *all* of the enemy's power. All! (Luke 10:19). The devil does not have authority or dominion over Christians unless it is given to him. The believer has authority and dominion over him, praise God! You can sit back and let the devil beat you up or you can stand against him in the power of the Lord Jesus Christ.

When Jesus ascended to the right hand of the Father, He sent us out to make disciples of all nations. He did not send us on our own though, He sent us with His power, His authority and His Spirit (Matthew 28:18-20). Praise God!

Jesus is now seated at the right hand of the Father, far above all rule, authority, power, domain and every title that can be given. That covers everything –*EVERYTHING!* God placed all things under his feet and appointed him to be head over everything for the church (Ephesians 1:19-23). Jesus is above all!

But it gets even better. Consider this exciting truth: God raised us up with Christ and seated us with Him in the heavenly realms (Ephesians 2:6-7). You are seated with Jesus in heavenly places! Satan is under the feet of Jesus. Satan is under your feet!

## THE ARMOUR OF GOD

We cannot enter the battlefield of the Christian journey without protection, as the enemy's flaming arrows come from all directions. A soldier does not enter the battlefield with his gun but no ammunition, or with ammunition but no gun. God's army needs the full armor of God so that it can take its stand against the devil's schemes.

Put on the *full* armor of God daily. Is the belt of truth buckled around your waist? Is the breastplate of righteousness in place? Are your feet fitted with the readiness that comes from the gospel of peace? Do you carry the shield of faith so you can extinguish the flaming arrows of the evil one? Is your helmet of salvation in place and the sword of the Spirit in hand? (Ephesians 6:10-17).

The devil waits for opportune moments to ambush. He is not polite in announcing sneak attacks. Satan arrives on the scene uninvited and at the most inconvenient times. God's armor enables you to stand your ground against the enemy every time. Do not hang up your armor for even a moment!

## THE NAME OF JESUS

The Name of Jesus explodes with power! God exalted Jesus to the highest place and gave him the Name that is above every name. At the Name of Jesus *every* knee must bow, in heaven and on earth and below the earth (Philippians 2:9-10). Anything with a name must bow to the name of Jesus!

The Name of Jesus sends the enemy scurrying. You have authority to use the Name of Jesus, praise God! You can boldly stand in the authority of the Name of Jesus and say, "NO!" to the devil, and he must obey. He has no choice because He must bow to the Name of Jesus.

How sad it would be if you were bequeathed a million-dollar inheritance but were unaware it had been deposited into your account. Without knowledge of your inheritance, you would suffer a poverty-stricken life even though all of your needs could be met through your abundant inheritance.

Likewise, your inheritance in Christ includes authority over the devil but it will be of no benefit unless you utilize it. Many Christians are beat up by the devil because they lack knowledge of the authority they possess in Christ.

Delve into the Word of God and study your authority in Christ! Know and exercise your God-given authority over the devil. The devil and his cohorts recognize your authority as a believer in Jesus Christ of Nazareth. Don't fear Satan. He fears you! He knows the greater One lives inside of you (1 John 4:4). The devil knows you are armed with the Sword of the Spirit and have the authority to use the Name of Jesus. The Name of Jesus sends the devil fleeing as in terror. The blood of Jesus is against Satan!

## SUBMIT YOURSELF TO GOD

The more you submit your life to Christ, the greater of a threat you become to the devil. To effectively exercise authority over the evil one, you must be completely submitted to God. James 4:7 says, "Submit yourselves, then, to God. Resist the devil, and he will flee from you." Sometimes Christians try to resist the devil before fulfilling their part in submitting themselves to God. Submit yourself to God by obeying God, *then* you can effectively resist the devil.

If you are not living according to the Bible or are in rebellion against God, you are not submitted to Him. If disobedient to God's teachings, wearing a Christian badge but living contrary to God's Word, you are not submitted to God.

Refusal to submit to God opens the door to the enemy. Satan sneaks through any door, even if opened a crack. If not wholly submitted to God and His Word, your authority as a believer is weakened and ineffective. Submit yourself to God first, *then* you can confidently resist the devil.

Remaining in fellowship with God and living according to His ways disables the devil from penetrating your life with his destructive demonic force. Obeying God's Word by acting on the Word of God builds a divine supernatural protection no enemy can break through. The devil is no match for the Creator of the universe. He is a loser in the life of a lover and follower of Jesus. The greater One lives in you!

As you succeed at pushing back the gates of hell, do not be surprised when the enemy does not back off. Satan relentlessly continues efforts to destroy anything associated with the kingdom of God. When he loses in one arena, he tries to steer you off course using an alternate avenue. He knows your weaknesses and seizes every available opportunity to tempt you in those weak areas. His strongest attacks arrive when he finds you in moments of weakness. Regardless of how great the temptation is, God always provides a way out for you (1 Corinthians 10:13). God will *always* send help.

Do not fear Satan, but be cognizant of his tactics and schemes. As you cling to God, you can discern and confront the enemy's tactics. By staying in constant communion with God, you avoid the risk of becoming spiritually dull and unable to recognize Satan's strategies.

Strife, division, destruction, and heartache are the enemy's calling card. Nothing he attempts to bring against you will succeed when you keep your eyes focused on Jesus. Nothing! "No weapon formed against you shall prosper" (Isaiah 54:17, NKJV). Satan cannot win with a child of God as Jesus already won the victory for

His children. God works wonders and goes to extreme measures to protect His children and to fulfill His promises to them.

## OUR DEFENSIVE WEAPON – THE SWORD OF THE SPIRIT

God provided a powerful defensive weapon for dealing with the devil, the same weapon Jesus used against the enemy: God's Word. The Sword of the Spirit wards off the enemy every time. When the devil stirs up trouble, this explosive weapon overcomes him and his works.

Have symptoms of sickness or disease attacked your body? Get out the Sword of the Spirit and boldly confess, "It is written: Jesus Himself took my infirmities and bore my sicknesses!" Are your finances under attack? Proclaim, "It is written: The blessings of Abraham are mine!" Regardless of what attacks come against you, find Scripture addressing your situation and confess it in the Name of Jesus. Confess it out loud, where the enemy hears you loud and clear. Then stand firm!

Meditate on and speak God's Word daily to deeply root it in your spirit. Faith comes from hearing; continually hearing the Word increases faith (Romans 10:17). Confession of Scripture builds faith and prepares you for demonic attacks. Read the Word, believe the Word, meditate on the Word, speak the Word and be a doer of the Word!

Do not wait until you develop cancer to build faith for healing. Study healing Scriptures from the Bible now. Confess what God says about your life instead of confessing what your circumstances dictate. You are healthy, prosperous, and victorious according to God's Word. As you speak the Word of God into your circumstances and choose to walk by faith, God's promises will rise above your circumstances in victory. The devil and his demonic attack will flee! Praise God, the Word works.

## WALKING IN LOVE

Walking in love is a strategic defensive weapon to effectively ward off the enemy. Satan focuses on bringing strife and division in every arena, putting much effort into breaking up marriages, splitting relationships, and dividing the body of Christ. God's love combats division and strife.

Opportunity for conflict presents itself daily. Allowing wounded emotions to reign leads to disaster, but allowing love to reign promotes spiritual freedom and victory. The enemy works hard at enticing us to respond to conflict with hostility, unforgiveness, anger and hatred. Don't allow it!

To reflect the image of Jesus Christ, respond to evil with blessing (1 Peter 3:9). To repay evil with evil is Satan's way. To repay evil with good is God's way. Choose God's way!

Responding to evil with love is a choice that requires crucifying the flesh. We need divine help to love those who do evil because our flesh naturally desires to repay evil with evil. Returning good for evil causes the devil to flee and keeps you in right standing with God. Send the enemy into confusion by doing the opposite of what he expects. Loving those who offend you is not an easy choice; it is the right choice.

As you extinguish Satan's flaming arrows by walking in love daily, you will be blessed, those around you will be blessed and God will be pleased as you act on His Word. The enemy loses the battle when you choose to love.

## TESTS AND TRIALS

Christians face trials of many kinds while on this earth. This truth comes as a big surprise to those who ignorantly view Christianity as a life of bliss, free from any kind of pain or suffering. *All* believers face the possibility of being thrown into a fiery furnace of trial when they least expect it. To come out of the fiery trials of life unharmed, you must follow God's plan for deliverance. Looking to God ushers in the victory regardless of how disastrous or life-threatening the trial is.

Satan often gets blamed for challenges believers face. Tests and trials are not always an assignment from the devil, although Satan is happy to take the credit. The devil certainly takes advantage of every opportunity to bring destruction, strife, and division in marriages, families and churches but cannot be blamed for all of our troubles.

Every Christian faces trial at one time or another. God never promised us a trial-free life. Some trials are simply part of God maturing us and testing our faith, and others are the result of our own error or disobedience. Let's look at the issue of tests and trials a bit further as it is an area many Christians struggle with.

Yes, trials come for many reasons. God warned us of many coming troubles, yet promised to deliver us from every one of them. Not some of them, all of them. *All!* (Psalm 34:19). Although we cannot dictate to God when or how He will deliver us, we can be confident that *we surely will be delivered.* Victory is always ours in Christ Jesus (Romans 8:37, NKJV).

The devil's attempts to steal, kill and destroy will not end until he is cast into the lake of fire, but we serve a great God who goes ahead of the schemes of the devil and makes the way for the victory. No matter what we face, victory is just around the corner.

The devil tries to convince us to throw in the towel before the victory comes and wants us to feel hopelessly defeated. Extinguish his efforts by keeping your eyes on the victory. When flaming arrows come your way, take up the shield of faith to extinguish every one (Ephesians 6:16). Stand firm! Victory is on the way!

Unfortunately, because trials are uncomfortable, we often rush to find a way to get out of the tough spots. *God, get me out of this!* echoes into the heavens. Instead of desperately trying to escape trial, take time to discover the hidden gold that may be disguised in the trial. We grow in the tough spots if we remain submitted to God! Trials are stepping stones to our destination. Some of life's most prosperous times of spiritual growth are birthed through trials we walk through with God.

Faith strengthens you through trial and propels you to victory. Note what Jesus told Simon Peter: "Satan has asked to sift you as wheat. But I have prayed for you, Simon, that your faith may not fail" (Luke 22:31). Jesus did not pray for Simon Peter's trial to be taken away, but instead prayed that his faith would not fail him. What a tremendous example for us! Satan may want to sift you as wheat too. Don't let your faith fail you! It is an opportunity to grow.

## JUST PASSING THROUGH!

It is not God's plan for you to stay in the midst of trial permanently. You are just *passing through* – don't park and shut off the engine.

Isaiah 43:2 says, "When you pass *through* the waters, I will be with you; and when you pass *through* the rivers, they will not sweep over you. When you walk *through* the fire, you will not be burned; the flames will not set you ablaze." You are just passing through; don't set up camp! Walk the trial out, don't sit down and quit before the victory comes!

Trusting God as you pass through the trials of life opens a continuous fountain of joy and peace. Keeping confidence in God enables you to continue enjoying life and bearing fruit right in the midst of the most difficult circumstances. Jeremiah 17:7-8 says, "Blessed is the man who trusts in the Lord, whose confidence is in him. He will be like a tree planted by the water that sends out its roots by the stream. It does not fear when heat comes; its leaves are always green. It has no worries in a year of drought and never fails to bear fruit." Are your leaves green? Are you bearing fruit as you pass through trials? Trusting God through trial enables you to travel the steady road of peace instead of the rough roller coaster ride of fear and anxiety.

## TRIALS CAN BE TESTS OF FAITH

Your darkest moments test faith and reveal faith. God uses trials as a method of revealing what is in your heart. God led the Israelites in the desert for forty years to humble them and to test them. He wanted to know what was in their hearts and wanted to see if they would keep his commands (Deuteronomy 8:2). Their trial in the wilderness was quite telling. What does God find in your heart during trial?

Tests and trials are learning and growing times for those desiring to mature in their faith. James 1:2-4 tells us, "Consider it pure joy, my brothers, whenever you face trials of many kinds, because you know that the testing of your faith develops perseverance. Perseverance must finish its work so you may be mature and complete, not lacking anything." Consider it pure joy, my friend, in the end you will be mature and complete!

Peter reminds us that faith is proved genuine through trials: "In this you greatly rejoice, though now for a little while you may have had to suffer grief in all kinds of trials. These have come so that your faith – of greater worth than gold, which perishes even though refined by fire – may be proved genuine and may result in praise, glory and honor when Jesus Christ is revealed" (1 Peter 1:6-7). Don't rejoice *about* the trials – rejoice *in* the trial! Try facing trials with joy instead of running in terror in the other direction. Adjust your attitude and allow God to use your trials to help you grow. If you stay submitted to God through trial, He won't waste your pain and suffering, but will bring good out of it.

Trials are opportunities to develop a deeper faith! Standing in faith and living in obedience to God's commands during the good times is no challenge, but standing in faith in the midst of trials locates us spiritually. When you are squeezed, what comes out?

## FREED IN THE FIRE

Life's most severe trials can arrive unexpectedly, even while we are in the midst of God's perfect will, serving Him with all of our heart, soul and strength. In the story of Shadrach, Meshach and Abednego (Daniel 3) lies some enlightening truth about trials.

Shadrach, Meshach and Abednego demonstrated an unyielding commitment to faithfully serve the one and only true God. In the midst of living a righteous life, they suddenly found themselves facing a life-threatening situation. They faced the fiery furnace of trial.

King Nebuchadnezzar set up an image of gold and commanded the people to bow down and worship the image. Anyone refusing to obey the King's command would immediately be thrown into a blazing furnace. Shadrach, Meshach and Abednego were unyielding to these instructions as they worshipped only the One true God. Nebuchadnezzar was furious and warned them that should they not change their mind, they would be thrown immediately into a blazing furnace.

Shadrach, Meshach and Abednego were confident their God could rescue them and made it clear that even if God did not rescue them, they would not serve the King's gods or worship the image of gold he had set up. Even facing possible death, they refused to bow down to anyone other than the One and only true God.

Following through with his expressed warning, King

Nebuchadnezzar had Shadrach, Meshach and Abednego tied up and thrown into the blazing furnace. Looking into the furnace, the King witnessed a miracle! He knew only three men were thrown into the flames, yet saw four men walking around in the fire – unbound – the fourth was the Lord.

Astounded at the sight, the King beckoned Shadrach, Meshach and Abednego to come out of the furnace. He discovered the fire had not harmed them – not a hair was singed, and their robes were not scorched. Not even a hint of the smell of smoke clung to them!

King Nebuchadnezzar decreed that anyone who spoke against the God of Shadrach, Meshach and Abednego would be cut into pieces and their homes be turned into piles of rubble. He testified that no other god could save in the way their God saved them. God delivered His faithful servants and received the glory for their deliverance. He will do the same for you!

God can miraculously set us free from bondage in the midst of a trial. Notice Shadrach, Meshach and Abednego faced their trial in bondage. Their hands were *firmly* bound before they were thrown into the furnace. Consider what King Nebuchadnezzar saw as he looked into the fiery flaming furnace! He saw they were *unbound* and unharmed (Daniel 3:25). Right in the midst of a blazing trial, they were set freed from the bondage that held them! Their fiery trial did not harm or destroy them, but it did destroy their bondage. They were set free!

God is doing much more than you realize through life's greatest challenges. By submitting to God in the midst of your mountainous trials, God can perform a mighty work in you and set you free from hidden things that bind you.

Can you trust God as Shadrach, Meshach and Abednego did? Can you allow Him to bring you to the places He can accomplish the work that needs to be done in you? Can you allow Him to work out of you what needs to be worked out in you? Can you allow Him to teach you the lessons you need to learn?

You may not understand why trials are happening, but you can be certain that in the end it will be good for you. God will make sure of it! Keeping your eyes focused on Jesus brings peace and confidence that one way or another, everything is going to be okay (Isaiah 26:3).

For gold to be purified, it must endure a refining process at extremely high temperatures. As the heat increases, the dross (waste matter) rises to the top, leaving pure gold behind. We, being purified as gold, must allow our refining process in the fiery trials of life. As the dross of our life rises to the top, may our Lord and Savior wipe it away to find His reflection. Victory awaits us in the midst of the fiery furnace. Choose to find the victory!

## PICK YOURSELF UP AND STAND

When facing trial, be certain of one thing: God's Word is truth and unchangeable. God, His Word and His promises are not invalidated when you are in the midst of trial. Circumstances and factual evidence are subject to change at any moment. God's Word, however, is settled forever, is unchangeable and stands firm in the heavens. It is the same yesterday, today and forever.

Follow the example of Shadrach, Meshach and Abednego. In the midst of trial, stand firm and refuse to bow down to circumstances that lure you to take your eyes off Jesus. The world takes note when you refuse to bow down to your trials. Your faith during trials is a powerful witness to the unbelieving world.

Have you suffered a spiritual setback? Stand up, soldier of Christ! Take your position of authority obtained for you through the blood of Jesus. Have you been beaten down or feel you failed God? Your Almighty Commanding Officer wants you to rise up. The time is short and He has work for you to accomplish on the earth. God's gifts and His calling are still yours (Romans 11:29). God needs you in His army, mighty child of the Living God. Get up, shine up your armor and stand. It's time to press on!

# CHAPTER 10
# The Love Walk

### GOD IS LOVE

Love is the very core of God. He *is* love. The Apostle John writes, "Dear friends, let us love one another, for love comes from God. Everyone who loves has been born of God and knows God. Whoever does not love does not know God, because God is love" (1 John 4:7-8). Out of His great love for us God sent His precious and only Son so we would not perish but instead would enjoy everlasting life (John 3:16). God is motivated by His unending love for us. We must be motivated by love as well.

Love is the main staple for the successful Christian journey and is the key to fulfilling your destiny in Christ. Maturing in your ability to love others accelerates your spiritual growth and allows you to flow in the abundant life God intended for you. The refusal or inability to love others, however, slows your growth to a screeching halt and causes you to become spiritually stagnant.

Establishing a life of love enables you to fulfill all of God's requirements. The ten commandments tell us not to commit adultery, not to murder, not to steal, not to covet, and a few other commands that are summed in one rule: Love your neighbor as yourself.

If you love your neighbor, you won't steal from him, you won't murder him, and you won't covet his spouse or cause him any harm. Love enables you to fulfill the entire law! (Romans 13:9-10). To please God, love must penetrate all areas of your life.

### GOD'S LOVE HAS BEEN POURED INTO YOUR HEART

Natural human love has severe limitations. On our own, we are incapable of loving the way God wants us to love. When we are born again, however, God pours His divine love into our hearts by the

133

Holy Spirit (Romans 5:5). Praise God, His love is resident within us! It is up to us, however, to release His love and to allow it to flow through our lives.

1 Corinthians 13:4-8 tells us of God's idea of love: "Love is patient, love is kind. It does not envy, it does not boast, it is not proud. It is not rude, it is not self-seeking, it is not easily angered, it keeps no record of wrongs. Love does not delight in evil but rejoices with the truth. It always protects, always trusts, always hopes, always perseveres. Love never fails."

God's idea of love is a tall order, isn't it? Are you capable of loving God's way? Absolutely, as He poured that ability to love into your heart by the Holy Spirit! God's love dwells within you.

The fruit of the Spirit operates through God's love. Galatians 5:22-23 highlights the fruit of the Spirit: Love, joy, peace, long suffering, gentleness, goodness, faith, meekness and temperance. It is not by chance that God listed love first as love must be present for the other spiritual fruit to operate.

Why does an apple tree produce fruit? Does it eat the fruit it produces? No! Those shiny, luscious apples are grown to bring nourishment to others. Likewise, as we grow in Christian maturity through a love-fueled life, we can produce a bumper crop of the fruit of the Spirit for those around us to partake of. The fruit in our lives is to bless others.

Many believers yearn for the power of God to flow through their lives. Miraculous healings, explosive miracles, and mountain-moving faith are sought after by many. The Kathryn Kuhlmans and Kenneth Hagins of the world discovered the key to this power and demonstrated it throughout their ministries. What is the key? They purposed to practice God's principles of love, refusing to take offense and speaking the best of everyone, whether friend or foe.

By seeking to increase the fruit of the Spirit, especially love, God's power will naturally flow because a person full of love is a vessel God can work through. A love-motivated life demonstrates both the fruit of the Spirit and the power of God. Seek after love and you will find the power of God.

Mastering the operation of love doesn't happen overnight, but instead must be walked out day by day. Choosing to operate in love is a daily choice. In fact, it's an hour by hour choice.

A Christian can give a grand appearance of being in right standing with God. He may give generously, memorize and confess an abundance of scripture, practice faith that brings about miracles and even operate in the gifts of the Holy Spirit – but if he is not able to love his brothers, his actions are insignificant. 1 Corinthians 13:1-3 says, "If I speak in the tongues of men and of angels, but have not love, I am only a resounding gong or a clanging cymbal. If I have the gift of prophecy and can fathom all mysteries and all knowledge, and if I have a faith that can move mountains, but have not love, I am nothing. If I give all I possess to the poor and surrender my body to the flames, but have not love, I gain nothing." Love is important to God.

I once followed a recipe for a delicious double layer chocolate cake. After gathering the ingredients, I carefully followed each step of the instructions, hoping to bless my family with a special treat for dessert. Much to my dismay, after baking and cooling the cake, it fell apart when I tried to remove it from the pans. Desperate to fix my mistake, I tried piecing the disastrous cake together, but it was a hopeless endeavor.

In reviewing the recipe, I realized I had inadvertently missed a key ingredient – the eggs. Although all other ingredients were included and the instructions were carefully followed, the cake could not be a success without the eggs.

Life in Christ can also be filled with numerous good ingredients while most of God's instructions are followed. But if we omit the main ingredient of love, we cannot attain abundant Christian life, as it is impossible to have God's best without love. Just as I tried to piece my fallen cake together without success, we cannot successfully complete our journey in Christ without love. We cannot survive without love flowing through our lives, as a loveless life eventually causes us to become spiritually shipwrecked.

## CHRISTIANS ARE KNOWN BY THEIR LOVE

Christians are not known as Jesus' disciples because they attend church on Sunday morning. They are not identified as His disciples because they talk about God and their faith in Him either. Christians do not belong to Christ because they wear a cross around their neck. They are not known as His disciples because they *say* they are His disciples and label themselves "Christian." Jesus claimed that all men would know His disciples by their love, one for another (John 13:35). You are identified as a follower of Christ by your demonstration of love. Your love walk exposes your identification in Christ.

Your demonstration of love for others is an undeniable witness to the world. The unbelieving world pays close attention to your actions and listens carefully to your words. Unloving actions often speak so loud that the world cannot hear words of love.

Have you ever told your neighbor about the love of Jesus in one breath, then gossiped about another neighbor down the street in the next breath? Do you share the gospel with people outside of your home yet bring disrespect and dishonor to your spouse or children inside your home? Are your actions confirming your words or contradicting them? Actions have a loud voice.

Jesus wants us to love one another, *as He loved us*. How sobering a thought. Meditating on God's love gives us a glimpse of what He is asking of us. Jesus' shed blood enabled us to be forgiven for all sin against God. Jesus gave His life for us long before we ever knew His name. Oh, what love He demonstrated to us! We are to love *as* He loved.

What is love anyway? Is it saying "I love you" to our neighbor? Is love a set of words? Is love a feeling? Although loving words bring warmth to people around us, it must reach beyond words. Love chooses to put action to our words.

If we tell our neighbor we love him, yet do nothing when we see him in need, our words are empty. If we say we love our neighbor yet do nothing when we hear he is sick, our words are cheap. Words mean nothing if not followed with action. 1 John 3:17-18 says, "If anyone has material possessions and sees his brother in need but has no pity on him, how can the love of God be in him? Dear children, let us not love with words or tongue but with actions and in truth." Love in action impacts those around us, not love in words alone.

James shares the importance of love in action as well: "Suppose a brother or sister is without clothes and daily food. If one of you says to him, 'Go, I wish you well; keep warm and well fed,' but does nothing about his physical needs, what good is it?" (James 2:15-16). Yes, child of God, what good is it?

When my mother died, I flew to the Midwest to be with my family. The week was filled with funeral planning and, through God's grace, opportunities to minister to those who were hurting. Returning back home, the reality of Mom's death unexpectedly hit me. My precious Mother was gone. Unable to express the unfamiliar emotions flooding me, I mourned silently.

While I was still in a numb state, a woman I hardly knew arrived at my home with a gift she had made as an expression of love and sympathy: a little container filled with one serving of stew. As I received Cheryl's gift of love, God brought to my remembrance the woman who put her two mites into the offering plate (Luke 21:1-4). She gave the Lord all of what she had. Cheryl gave all of what she had as well. Her gift of stew ministered to me more than anything else did during my season of mourning. Acts of love you may consider insignificant can powerfully impact people more than you may realize.

We find special opportunities to love our neighbors in the midst of difficult trials. Well-meaning people commonly tell a hurting person, "Let me know if I can do something for you." Although this is a loving expression, people in pain are often either unable to express their needs or too emotionally numb to even know what they need.

What an opportune moment to ask the Holy Spirit to reveal their needs! A simple phone call with a word of encouragement, a card, or even a bowl of stew can make a tremendous difference in someone's life. Let your words of love become actions of love.

Tom once dressed up as a clown to entertain children at a church picnic. Although not made known to anyone, he suffered from a painful migraine headache. All afternoon children crowded around him, pulled his nose, squeaked his horn and grabbed the balloons he had carefully formed into animals.

While Tom continued tying balloons, a parent told him that a boy named Andrew had been hospitalized with a heart condition. She asked if he was willing to visit him.

137

As the church picnic wound down, Tom's pain was obvious in his strained eyes, although a faith-filled smile remained on his face. Leaving the church, he drove to the hospital to minister to Andrew. Pressing through his pain, Tom sowed joy into this young life, selflessly demonstrating God's love when he no doubt didn't feel like it. When I visited Andrew several days later, he talked endlessly about the funny clown that had visited him in the hospital. Tom's love made a difference in little Andrew's life.

Are you willing to demonstrate love to your neighbor? Demonstrating love for others often requires a sacrifice on your part. Being a vessel of God's love may require your time, your money, or your emotions. Are you willing?

## DO I HAVE TO LOVE THAT PERSON?

Jesus instructed us to love one another, not only those who are *easy* to love or those we *feel* like loving. Jesus tells us to love our enemies and to pray for those who persecute us (Matthew 5:43-44). We are called to do the hard thing, not the easy thing:

> If you love those who love you, what credit is that to you? Even 'sinners' love those who love them. And if you do good to those who are good to you, what credit is that to you? Even 'sinners' do that… But love your enemies, do good to them, and lend without expecting to get anything back. Then your reward will be great, and you will be sons of the Most High, because he is kind to the ungrateful and wicked. Be merciful, just as your Father is merciful (Luke 6:32-36).

Herein lies the challenge for Christians. Loving those who are kind to us, agree with us, look like us and act like us is easy. Unbelievers can love the loving with no problem, but disciples of Christ must be different. Jesus taught us to love our enemies; those who hurt us, persecute us, and go out of their way to make our lives miserable.

Regardless of what our neighbor does to us, we are not excused from loving him. We are not required to be his best friend, and we don't necessarily have to like him or his actions, but we must love him with the love of the Lord. Loving him will demonstrate to him, and the world, that we are disciples of Jesus Christ.

John shares the sobering reality: "If anyone says, 'I love God,' yet hates his brother, he is a liar. For anyone who does not love his brother, whom he has seen, cannot love God, whom he has not seen. And he has given us this command: Whoever loves God must also love his brother" (1 John 4:20-21). *Whoever loves God must also love his brother.* God is clear. You cannot hate your brother and love God at the same time. If you say you love God yet do not love your neighbor, God calls you a liar. Ouch!

Some tell God, "But Lord… He's such a jerk… I just can't love him… He hurt me so badly." Yes, you *can* love that person as God gave you the ability to love him through the love He poured into your heart. Choose to love him. Love is a choice.

God will test your love walk throughout life. Choosing to love, especially the unlovable, is one of the most important choices you will ever make. Although not an easy choice, love is a necessary choice. Yes, people will cross your path that are not easy to love, and without God's divine love flowing through you, you will unlikely succeed in loving them. Allowing God's love to flow in your life will enable you to love the worst enemy. Choose to pass the love test!

## WEEDS IN THE GARDEN OF YOUR HEART

A beautiful garden filled with color crayon tulips and fragrant lilies borders our front yard. To maintain its beauty and to encourage flourishing plants, I invest much time and effort into weeding. Failing to weed on a regular basis causes the garden's beauty to quickly fade and leaves it drab and unkempt. Weeding is hard but necessary work.

Weeds are stubborn. When pulling a weed, the stem often breaks off, leaving the root still deeply implanted in the soil. If I do not dig the root out, the weed reappears within days and the process begins again. I often dig deep into the soil to eradicate the entire root as the deeper the root is implanted, the more difficult it is to get it out. Roots are deceiving; what sometimes appears as a tiny little weed above the soil has a root more than a foot long.

Weeds spring up in the garden of our hearts when love grows

cold. A cold heart invites bitterness to take root. If the root of bitterness is not uprooted, it will resurface and rear its ugly head again and again, bringing increasing destruction every time.

Like a weed, the deeper the root of bitterness is implanted in our heart, the more difficult it is to purge from our life. The root of bitterness can be deceiving. A Christian can have a cheerful smile on his face while harboring a grudge toward someone in his heart. A deep root of bitterness is not always apparent on the surface, but eventually its presence becomes obvious.

Weeding the garden of our hearts is necessary to remain spiritually flourishing and attractive. Just as I cannot avoid new weeds appearing in my garden, we cannot avoid facing opportunities for weeds of bitterness to take root in our heart. We must choose to lay hurts at the feet of Jesus before they take root in our heart. Have you weeded your garden lately?

## THE DEVIL'S BAIT

Bitterness, unforgiveness, and hatred constipate the spiritual life of the believer. These destructive forces are birthed through the devil's deceptive trap of offense. Opportunities arrive every day for offense; nobody is immune from offense.

Growing up in the Midwest, we often fished for recreation. We'd string fat night crawlers on the hook for bait. After casting the line out, that juicy worm wiggled around, enticing nearby fish to a tasty meal. Unable to resist, some unsuspecting fish chomped the worm, not realizing a fatal hook lurked underneath it. Then, of course, he is snared, dragged in and eaten for dinner.

Offenses are the devil's bait. Satan sets traps of offense, dangling irresistible morsels of hurts, emotional wounds, jealousy, and misunderstandings in front of you. If you take Satan's bait of offense, he wastes no time in reeling you into his snare. Once hooked, bitterness, unforgiveness and hatred begin to eat away at your destiny in Christ. That juicy little morsel of offense can become a destructive force capable of eroding numerous areas of your life.

Be aware of the danger of offense! Satan's bait, initially appearing as a small offense, can transform into a monstrous roadblock of disaster. When born, offenses cry to be nursed into bitterness. If bitterness is fed, it rapidly grows into unforgiveness like a malignant tumor, poisoning your entire being.

As you think about, talk about, and meditate on offenses, they become bigger, dominating your thought life and stealing joy. If not arrested, offenses continue spreading with a vengeance until your life is saturated with bitterness. Consumed with the consequences of offense, a lack of peace, an inability to pray, and no sense of God's presence are evident.

The devil wants to steal your joy, peace and destiny through offense. Have you allowed him to steal from you? Is your joy gone? Check out your love walk.

Other people may become offended and want to share their offense with you. Refuse to take on other people's offenses! "Well, I can't help it if someone tells me something," some say. Yes, you can! You can lovingly refuse to take part in listening to the gossip resulting from other people's offenses. Don't get dragged into other people's strife. Be careful of how you listen (Luke 8:18). What you hear affects you more than you may realize.

Offenses are poisonous and deadly. If offered poison, you would refuse it, wouldn't you? When offered offense, simply refuse to take it. Offenses bring death and destruction just as poison does. Treat offenses like the plague and stay as far away from them as you possibly can. Fill up with love daily and leave no room for offenses!

Are you poisoning others with your offenses? "Well, it's just my spouse, I tell him everything," or, "I'm just sharing it with other people so they can pray about it." Be careful, Christian friend, those excuses are a snare of the enemy. You poison others by gossiping about offenses.

Learning to deal with offense is one of the most challenging areas Christians face. Because staying free of offense does not come naturally, the first thing many people are tempted to do when offended is talk about, think about, and react to the offense. Being led by the Holy Spirit instead of being led by the flesh will enable you to conquer these challenges. It requires hard work to stay free from offense. *Anything* you purpose to master takes hard work.

If anyone had reason to take offense, Jesus did. God in the flesh, Jesus was a perfect sinless man. He continually demonstrated selfless unconditional love, yet those he tried to help sent him to the cross. Those he came to heal and set free yelled, "Crucify Him!"

Jesus had more reason to be offended than we will ever have; yet He chose not to be offended. Although Jesus was the Son of God, He was also human, so I suspect he was tempted to be offended, don't you think? Instead of taking offense, He asked God to forgive those who crucified Him. Striving to have a conscience without offense toward God and men (Acts 24:16), purpose every day to stay free from offense!

Heed a great truth spoken by King Solomon: "He who covers offenses seeks love" (Proverbs 17:9). Every offense that comes your way is an opportunity to seek love. Turn from the evil of offense and go the other direction to seek and pursue peace (Psalm 34:14). It's your choice to make.

## THE CANCER OF UNFORGIVENESS

No human being is any different from the next when it comes to being hurt or offended. Not a soul on earth has been spared from deep emotional wounds at one time or another. Other Christians may hurt you. Church leadership may treat you wrongfully. Loved ones may gossip about you. Maybe you have been wounded by strangers, teachers, parents, your own children, or a trusted mentor. Have you suffered a wound inflicted by an anointed man or woman of God? The sting of offense is painful.

Your response to offense is critical. Wounded emotions must be taken to the feet of Jesus. They must be taken to the cross where healing flows freely.

The cancer of unforgiveness will not leave on its own. You must choose to get rid of unforgiveness by forcing it to leave. Paul instructs, "Be kind and compassionate to one another, forgiving each other, just as in Christ God forgave you" (Ephesians 4:32). Forgive others *just as* God forgave you. Do you remember how Jesus forgave you? He forgave it all – every single sin you have committed or will commit. *No exceptions.* You are to forgive like Jesus forgave.

You are not excused from forgiving any offense. Let's face it, choosing to forgive is not always easy, especially when you claim justifiable reasons not to forgive. Maybe your offender does not want to be forgiven; maybe he hasn't even acknowledged doing anything wrong or doesn't care if he did. Maybe the wound was intentionally inflicted. Emotional wounds can mount, touching every area of your life. If obsessed with the pain, you sink lower and lower into spiritual quicksand as bitterness closes you in, squeezing the very breath out of you.

Your emotional wounds may manifest in physical pain, yet your offender continues to refuse to apologize. The stark reality is that you may never get an apology. Your offender may have even died long ago but the hurt he caused lives on. God does not excuse you from forgiving under any circumstances. He does not limit forgiveness only to those who ask for forgiveness, but instead tells you to forgive as He forgave. His forgiveness is limitless. He died and took the punishment for your sins long before you ever said you were sorry.

If you wait until you *feel* like forgiving, you may never do it. You cannot determine whether or not you will forgive based on your offender's response or lack of response either. Soak in God's Word on the subject of forgiveness, then *choose* to forgive based on the Word of God, not on how you feel. Forgiving God's way will set you free!

Missing out on forgiveness will cause you to miss out on heaven. How sobering the words of Jesus: "If you forgive men when they sin against you, your heavenly Father will also forgive you. But if you do not forgive men their sins, your Father will not forgive your sins" (Matthew 6:14-15). Oh, the seriousness of unforgiveness. If you refuse to forgive, you will not be forgiven. Where will you be then?

Instead of holding on to and nursing unforgiveness, choose to forgive your offender regardless of what he did. Letting go of bitterness will not only set your offender free, but, more importantly, will set you free from the deadly consequences of unforgiveness. It requires humility to forgive someone who may not deserve forgiveness. Jesus offered you forgiveness when you were undeserving, how can you refuse to forgive others?

Humbling yourself through forgiveness cultivates spiritual maturity. Can you humble yourself to the point of asking God to forgive your offender, or are you afraid he will get away with what he did? Can you ask God not to hold the offense against him? That is exactly what Jesus did as He hung on the cross so you could be forgiven. Can you follow His example?

Unforgiveness thrusts you into the enemy's territory. The destructive force of unforgiveness can lead to sickness, disease and premature death, all destructive forces abundant in Satan's territory. Unforgiveness steals God's blessings and keeps you out of God's will. If the blessings of God are not flowing in your life, humble yourself and ask God to expose any hidden places of hurt.

Walking in love allows you to fly like the eagles, free from the bondage of unforgiveness and bitterness. Free yourself from baggage you have carried around for days or years. Has that little pebble of offense you picked up long ago grown into a monstrous boulder? Lay down the extra baggage that burdens you. Choose to love!

Take a moment right now to examine your heart. Are you harboring a grudge against someone? Is there bitterness or unforgiveness in your heart? Be honest with yourself and ask God to reveal those hidden areas to you. Christian friend, take your wounds to the cross.

The miracle you may be waiting for is hinged to your ability to forgive. Faith works by love (Galatians 5:6). Without love, faith will not work. Regardless of how many faith confessions you make – it will not work.

Releasing forgiveness is the last thing the devil wants you to do, as he knows that if he can stop you from forgiving, he can squelch your blessings. The evil one wants you to harbor grudges and will provoke you to dwell in unforgiveness. Satan hates it when you choose to love by extending forgiveness. Love covers the sin that Satan wants to keep exposed (1 Peter 4:8).

## HOW CAN I FORGIVE?

How do you forgive when you simply feel incapable of forgiving? The first step is often the greatest hurdle: Making the choice to forgive. Be honest with God. If necessary, admit that although you confess forgiveness with your mouth, you really don't feel it in your heart. God can handle it; He already knows it anyway! Ask God to help you. He is faithful.

By allowing God's love to flow through you, the Great Physician's touch will heal your wounded heart. Just as gaping physical wounds take time to heal, wounded hearts take time to heal. Your choice to forgive enables the healing process to begin. Allow yourself time to heal.

To accelerate freedom in forgiveness, take love action. Can you take a step of faith by demonstrating an expression of love to your offender? In the flesh this is not an easy task, but the eternal rewards are limitless.

A Christian woman once wounded me unexpectedly. Having little experience in relationship strife, the situation paralyzed me for days. Emotionally numbed, I had no understanding of the reasoning behind her hurtful actions.

After taking the situation to God in search of wisdom for my response, He told me exactly what I didn't want to hear at the time. *Forgive her.* Out of obedience to God, I purposed to reach beyond my hurting emotions to offer forgiveness. After choosing to forgive and asking God not to hold her actions against her, I still didn't feel any better. Every time I saw my forgiven offender, the ache in the pit of my stomach reminded me that my wounds were still healing.

Led by God to put action to my forgiveness, I approached my offender, wrapped my arms around her and said, "I love you." Her arms hung at her sides; she remained silent and expressionless. Although her response was negative, I walked away knowing my shackles of unforgiveness had been loosened. Feeling sudden compassion, I hoped that my intentional expression of love would somehow free her from any guilt she may suffer. Regardless of her response, I found freedom.

Is it easy to express love to the person who caused much suffering? No! But the steps of loving action will salve your wounds and expedite the healing process. Romans 12:18 says "If it is possible as far as it depends on you, live at peace with everyone."

Are there steps you could take to live at peace with someone? Take those steps. Forgiveness in action will enable you to take a giant leap in spiritual growth and will cause the feelings of forgiveness to catch up to your confession of forgiveness.

Does your offender know he is forgiven? Do your actions

demonstrate forgiveness? Do you say, "Oh yes, I've forgiven brother so and so," yet you refuse to speak to him? Have you already confronted and resolved an issue with your offender, yet continually remind him of his mistake? If you truly forgave him, you will not continue to bring the offense to his attention. Overcome the temptation to rehearse the offense in your mind or to repeat it with your mouth. Do not bring the offense up again – ever – to anyone.

Have you been pained by hearing others rave about the wonderful qualities of someone who intentionally wronged you? Has your flesh risen up, tempting you to scream, "Well, let me just tell you a thing or two about this person you feel is so wonderful!" How great the temptation can be to spill the beans. Be careful! Announcing and amplifying offenses only strips open your emotional wounds once again.

Silence your mouth! If past hurts surface, remind yourself, and the devil, that your offender is forgiven. Then move on. In time, the memory of the emotional wound will no longer have a hold on you. You will be freed from the prison of offense!

## WHAT FORGIVING IS NOT

*Forgiving does not mean the memory of the offense will be miraculously erased.* It is normal to have memory of past hurts. But dwelling and meditating on those hurts will keep you stuck in the mud of the past instead of allowing you to move into the future free from the bondage of bitterness. Allow yourself to have the memory of past hurts, but don't allow those memories to have you.

*Forgiving does not mean you excuse what your offender did.* Even though your offender is forgiven, he often faces natural consequences for his actions. Consequences always follow when one chooses to act out of God's will. For example, if a drunk driver hit and killed one of my children, he would likely face time in prison or whatever the law requires of him. Retribution is often in order as well. Although there is no excuse for taking my child's life, God would not excuse me from forgiving my child's killer.

*Forgiving does not mean you are required to continue a relationship.* Some relationships are simply not healthy relationships and should not continue. If trouble regularly comes into your life through an established relationship, exercise godly wisdom in seeking whether or not this relationship should continue. Forgiveness is always necessary, regardless of how you were wronged, yet a reestablishment of the relationship is not required.

## KEYS TO THE LOVE WALK

A Christian must heed God's instruction in addressing a brother who sins against him. It's simple. If a brother sins against you, go and show him his fault, but keep it just between the two of you (Matthew 18:15).

Too often a believer shares his dilemmas with other brothers and sisters instead of approaching his offender directly. Though he may eventually restore the relationship with his offender, he leaves behind a trail of bitterness and resentment among the people he blabbed his business to. Don't pull others into your issues by spreading your problems through the prayer chain!

If you find yourself in the midst of strife with another person, pray! The battle is not of the flesh, it is of the spirit and it must be dealt with in the spirit (Ephesians 6:12, KJV). Do battle through prayer, not through people. Find the power of God on your knees!

After taking authority in the spiritual realm, take any necessary action in the natural to bring peace with your brothers and sisters. Do everything within your power to live at peace with everyone (Romans 12:18). The enemy cowers as God's Word prevails.

## THE POWER OF THE TONGUE

To walk in love, one must learn to keep a rein on his tongue. This small part of the body has the power to speak life and death (Proverbs 18:21). Are your words building others up or tearing them down? Are you reacting to others with your mouth or slow to speak and responding in love? Ephesians 4:29 instructs us regarding the fruit of our mouth: "Do not let any unwholesome talk come out of your mouths, but only what is helpful for building others up according to their needs, that it may benefit those who listen."

Are your words benefiting those who listen to you? Jump on more opportunities to spread good reports instead of spreading anger and gossip! Tattle on people when you hear something positive about them. Don't miss an opportunity to build and encourage others.

Regardless of what words are spoken to you, choose to control your response. If someone attacks you verbally, extinguish that flaming arrow by responding in love. Love diffuses anger and can transform the worst of situations. A gentle answer turns away wrath (Proverbs 15:1). An easy task? No! But with God's help, you can put a guard over your mouth and keep watch over the door of your lips (Psalm 141:3). It takes practice!

Although you may look pretty on the outside with a flashing smile, your mouth gives you away. Your heart's condition is exposed through your words. If good treasure is in your heart, good treasure comes out of your mouth. If evil treasure is in your heart, evil treasure comes out of your mouth (Luke 6:45). What kind of treasure is escaping your mouth from your heart?

Have you ever spotted a spiritually mature person who practices walking in love? He bubbles over with joy! He enjoys liberty and freedom through love. You too can possess freedom and liberty. Consider letting a car ahead of you in the traffic; open the door for an elderly person; give a hurting friend a hug; make a phone call to the one weighing on your heart; apologize to your wounded relative; visit the neighbor who faces marital problems; smile at a stranger; cry with a brother or sister in mourning. Little acts of love can make a tremendous impact on other people's lives and you get blessed in the process. King Solomon knew the key: If you refresh others, you will be refreshed as well (Proverbs 11:25).

Be a vessel of love ready to be used of God at any time and in any place. Ask God to lead you to someone needing the love of Christ. Seize the moment to love, as you may be the only Jesus that person ever sees. Purpose in your heart to go out of your way for someone every day. God prepared opportunities in advance for you to show the love of Jesus (Ephesians 2:10) – be on the lookout! Whether at the grocery store, the office, or the church, endless opportunities to demonstrate love await you.

As you walk in love daily, be cognizant of the needs and interests of others. Philippians 2:3-4 tells us, "In humility consider others better than yourselves. Each of you should look not only to your own interests, but also to the interests of others." Develop a habit of thinking of the needs and interests of others instead of only thinking of yourself and your own needs.

Notice the Apostle Paul does not tell us to be a doormat though. Paul does not tell us to think *only* of others and not of ourselves, but instead to look at our own interests *as well as* other people's interests.

Loving others is not optional for blood bought Christians but commanded by the King of Kings and the Lord of Lords. Heed the Words of the King: "As you have heard from the beginning, his command is that you walk in love" (2 John 6).

Let God breathe life into your Christian journey through His heartbeat of love. Open the gate of your heart and walk your journey in Christ out day by day, child of God. Walk it out in love.

# CHAPTER 11
# Touching His Throne With Prayer

**ENTRANCE INTO THE HOLY OF HOLIES**

The sacrifice of Jesus and the blood He shed enables us to enter into God's presence in the Holy of Holies (Hebrews 10:19-22). Our Creator, the Creator of the universe, says, "Come, my child." We can enter into His glorious presence!

God is touchable! He is Jehovah Shammah, the Lord that is present. Powerful and mighty God desires a close, intimate relationship with you. The Creator of the universe yearns for fellowship with you. Halleluia! Jesus made the way for you to enjoy an open line of communication with God.

You can freely approach God's throne at any time and in any place. Because of His open door policy, you do not need an appointment; His schedule is always free. In the busyness of a hectic day or the calm still of the night, God waits for you. Come *boldly* to His throne of grace (Hebrews 4:16). You gained the legal right to come boldly before the Father through the precious blood of Jesus. Praise God!

**ARE GOD'S CHILDREN IGNORING HIM?**

Have you spent time with your Father today? Have you showered God with your love? Have you thanked Him for His many blessings? Have you given God praise? Maybe you've been too busy.

How often I've made excuses for not praying. Although I intended to pray, I would sadly say, "I just didn't have time today. I guess the day got away from me." Yet, in looking over the day, I realized I made time to meet with a friend, to talk on the phone, and to complete a number of other activities, some of which had little value.

151

To cultivate an intimate relationship with God, we must give Him top priority instead of squeezing Him into our schedule with left over morsels of time. If we have no time for God, we are simply too busy and must consider re-evaluating our priorities. Jesus made fellowship with God through prayer a priority and it ought to be a priority for us as well. Is prayer a priority for you?

I profess to love my husband. How would Tom feel if I listened to tapes about him, read books about him, and spent all of my waking hours talking about how wonderful he is, yet never spent any time with him? What if I never talked to Tom and didn't share intimate time with him? It is impossible to enjoy a close personal relationship under those circumstances, yet this typifies many believers' relationship with God.

God wants you to know about Him, but desires even more for you to *know Him intimately*. An intimate relationship with God is cultivated by spending time in His presence. He promises to come near to you as you come near to Him (James 4:8).

As a mother, it brings me joy when my children talk to me about their life. I cherish hearing them say, "I love you, Mom." It lifts me up when they thank me for the things I do for them. It blesses me when they approach me with a need. It gives me great pleasure when they make special dates with me. It warms my heart to comfort them when they are hurting or sad. It touches me to hear them say, "I'm sorry, Mom," when they disappoint me.

As a Father, God yearns to spend time with His children. It brings your Daddy God joy to hear, "I love you." He likes to be thanked for what He does for you. It gives Him pleasure to take care of your needs. Your Father offers forgiveness when you say, "I'm sorry."

God is always thrilled when you make time for Him. His desire to be with you is so great that He gave His only Son, Jesus, to be sacrificed for your sin so you could be in His presence. The sacrifice of Jesus enables Him to hear your prayers and to be attentive to them (1 Peter 3:12). Has that sacrifice been taken for granted?

## LEARNING TO PRAY

Many Christians lack a prayer life simply because they do not know how to pray. Many want to pray but fear their words might not sound right. This is a common dilemma in the body of Christ.

I vividly remember the first Bible study I attended. After a large group teaching, we broke into smaller groups of fifteen to discuss the lesson. In closing the discussion, the leader instructed us to join hands to pray. One by one we were to pray out loud.

I panicked. *PRAY OUT LOUD*? I thought, *What am I going to say? I've never prayed out loud before and certainly have never prayed in front of anyone! Their prayers sound so perfect; I don't know what to say! Help!*

As each woman prayed, my nervous stomach continued to churn. My blank mind searched unsuccessfully for the right words to say when my dreaded turn came. I finally sputtered out a weak prayer with a trembling voice.

God revealed an area I needed to grow in as I recognized my need to overcome the fear of praying corporately. I realized, in fact, I really didn't know how to pray at all.

Determined to learn about prayer and to overcome my diffidence, I joined a women's prayer group. Although nervous and uncomfortable, I discovered this to be a safe environment to overcome my fear of praying. Faithfully attending weekly prayer meetings, I eventually became a prayer leader. Finding victory over fear, I found great reward in helping others learn to pray.

Many believers experience a lack of confidence in prayer or are intimidated to pray out loud simply because they have not learned how to pray. Just as you learned to read or write, you must also learn how to pray. Growth and maturity in prayer are key essentials to a victorious Christian journey.

You can see by the instructions Jesus gave, prayer should not be overwhelming or intimidating. Jesus instructed us in prayer, "When you pray, do not be like the hypocrites, for they love to pray standing in the synagogues and on the street corners to be seen by men. I tell you the truth, they have received their reward in full. But when you pray, go into your room, close the door and pray to your Father, who is unseen. Then your Father, who sees what is done in secret, will reward you. And when you pray, do not keep on babbling like pagans, for they think they will be heard because of their many words. Do not be like them, for your father knows what you need before you ask him" (Matthew 6:5-8).

God is not looking for fancy words or flowery prayers. He is looking for a child of God with a heart seeking after Him. Relax in His presence – He has no set agenda. Simply come to God and talk to Him.

## HOW SHOULD WE PRAY?

Although the various aspects of prayer could fill countless books, we will look at just a few key areas in the following pages. We will only scratch the surface of an element of the Christian life that must be studied and understood thoroughly. An effective prayer life can be birthed through consistent study of the instruction written in the Bible and a consistent practice of prayer.

Praise and Thanksgiving: When you pray, enter into God's presence with thanksgiving in your heart and praise in your mouth (Psalm 100:4). God is great and most worthy of praise (1 Chronicles 16:25). Entering His gates with praise and thanksgiving ushers in God's presence! Take time to bask in Almighty God's presence through praise and worship.

To Whom Do I Pray?: The Bible instructs us to pray to God the Father in the name of Jesus. We are not instructed to pray to dead relatives, saints, or to anyone other than our Father in heaven, in the name of Jesus. Jesus explains, "I tell you the truth, my Father will give you whatever you ask in my name. Until now you have not asked for anything in my name. Ask and you will receive, and your joy will be complete" (John 16:23-24). He confirms again, "I will do whatever you ask in my name, so that the Son may bring glory to the Father. You may ask me for anything in my name, and I will do it" (John 14:13-14).

Jesus is the *only* mediator between God and man (1 Timothy 2:5-6). Jesus is the *one and only* mediator. No alternative routes are available to the Father. Jesus is the only way (John 14:6). He is at the right hand of the Father interceding on our behalf right now (Romans 8:34).

Pray In Agreement with the Word of God: Effective prayer is in agreement with God's Word. As you get filled with God's Word by writing His Word on the tablet of your heart, your prayers will naturally revolve around His Word and His desires. Without knowledge of the Word of God, prayer can be ineffective, as God acts only in line with His Word, not in line with your desires that contradict His unchanging Word.

Just as you need food to promote physical health, God's Word keeps your spiritual health vibrant. A well-rounded spiritual diet consists of hearing, reading, studying, and meditating on God's Word. "Man does not live on bread alone, but on every word that comes from the mouth of God (Matthew 4:4). Are you feeding your spirit? In order to know the Word of God, you must feed on God's Word.

If ignorant of God's covenant promises revealed through His Word, you really cannot exercise faith as you pray because you have nothing to base your faith on. Don't take my word or someone else's word for what the Bible says! Discover for yourself what God provided so you can appropriate those provisions by faith.

Praying according to God's revealed will brings assurance that God hears your prayer and that you will receive whatever you asked of Him as well. Praise God, you can pray and *know* you received it! Hallelujah! Meditate on the exciting truth in 1 John 5:14: "This is the confidence we have in approaching God: that if we ask anything *according to his will*, he hears us. And if we know that he hears us – whatever we ask – we know that we have what we asked of him." We *know* we have what we asked of Him! We do not need to hope or wish for the best, we can *know*. We can expect it! The key, however, is *praying according to God's will*. Praying for anything that contradicts God's written Word wastes time because God *never* contradicts His Word.

Praying in line with God's Word allows us to take the "if" out of our prayers. Ending all prayers with, "if it be your will," is not praying in faith. Saying, "God, heal me… if it be your will" is ineffective prayer because God already made it clear that it is His will for you to be healed. Receive it!

There is a place for submitting to God's will in our lives but when we pray according to God's Word, we do not need to ask for His will because He already made His will known. If God promised something, there should be no "if" about it!

Before you bring a petition to the Lord, search Scripture to find the promises addressing your petition. Establish God's will through His Word and set your heart on those promises. Keep those Scriptures before your eyes and in your mouth as you stand in faith. Stay filled with the Word daily!

Pray in Faith: God moves mountains for those choosing to believe Him by faith. The Bible says, "Faith is the substance of things hoped for, the evidence of things not seen" (Hebrews 11:1, NKJV). Faith takes those things we hope for and pulls them into the natural realm!

Stand in faith for the promises of God. Stand *firm* on those promises regardless of your circumstances in the natural. Fight the good fight of faith (1 Timothy 6:12, NKJV). Appropriate the blessings of God by refusing to budge from your foundation of truth.

Walking by faith is not easy when visible circumstances appear contrary to God's promises. It feels unnatural to call things that are not as if they were, yet that is exactly what God wants you to do (Romans 4:17). Make the choice to grab hold of the Word and don't let go!

Answers to prayer may not be visible immediately but faith can stand in the gap until the answer is visible. If you believe it, you will see it (Matthew 21:22). Jesus said, "I tell you the truth, if anyone says to this mountain, 'Go, throw yourself into the sea,' and does not doubt in his heart but believes that what he says will happen, it will be done for him. Therefore I tell you, whatever you ask for in prayer, *believe that you have received it*, and it will be yours" (Mark 11:23-24).

Praise God, it *will be* yours! What a tremendous promise to stand on. Know, however, if out of fellowship with God, you cannot stand on this promise, or any promise for that matter. If in rebellion against God, His promises are not yours until you repent and turn your heart toward Him.

Notice that when you pray, the believing comes *before* the receiving, *not after*. It does not require faith to believe for something after you can see it, touch it, or feel it. See with the eye of faith, regardless of what you see in the natural. Christians are instructed to walk by faith, not by sight (2 Corinthians 5:7, NKJV).

If you prayed in faith and believe you received the answer when you prayed, stand in faith until the manifestation comes. When praying about the situation, instead of asking again and again, remind God of His Word and the promises He made regarding your request (Isaiah 43:26, NKJV). God honors His Word. Pray with expectancy. The answer is on the way!

People often beg God for provisions He made 2000 years ago at the cross of Calvary. Maybe you need to stop asking and start receiving what God already gave you. Are you waiting to give God praise and thanksgiving for the things He already purchased for you with His life? Are you waiting until you can see the answer? If you truly believe you received the answer when you prayed in faith, thank Him for the answer! Thanking and praising God before you see the answer to your prayer is an act of faith.

Pray With Expectation: Several years ago I prayed in faith for restoration of my eyesight. From the time I was a teen, my vision was poor and required corrective lenses for nearsightedness. After studying God's Word regarding His provision for the health of my body, I was fully persuaded it was His will for me to enjoy good vision. I believed keeping God's Word in the midst of my heart would bring health to my whole body (Proverbs 4:20-22)-including my eyes. I knew nothing was impossible for God (Luke 1:37) so restoring my vision was not a problem for God.

From the day I received my vision by faith, I continued thanking God for the restoration of my sight, although in the natural I could see no better. Following God's example, I called that which was not (perfect vision) as though it were and expected the manifestation of my healing every day.

As Tom and I climbed one of Seattle's scenic mountains one sunny afternoon, a furry yellow jacket was drawn to my perfume and began furiously buzzing around my head. This irritant continued circling me up the mountain until, much to my dismay, it flew right into my hair and stuck there!

Screaming, I frantically tried to shake the yellow jacket out of my hair. Realizing the pest was finally gone, I slowly opened my eyes and looked around in awe. I couldn't see! My vision was extremely blurry.

I had often daydreamed about my eyesight being restored and wondered what would happen if God restored my vision while I was wearing glasses or contact lenses. My vision would obviously be blurry, as the correction would no longer be needed.

Eyes blurry, I was dumbfounded as I stood on the side of the mountain. *What an odd time for God to heal my eyes!* I thought. Praise God though, I was thrilled!

My excitement quickly fizzled. Realizing that my glasses had flown off when I shook the bee out of my hair, my eyesight was blurry because my vision remained unchanged. I stood helpless, unable to see, while Tom searched for my glasses in the bushes. God surely must have chuckled at the sight.

Does the fact that my vision remained the same nullify God's Word? Does it indicate I will never see clearly? No! God's Word is truth and I continue to persevere. I expected the restoration of my eyesight as I went up that mountain and I continue to expect it now. As we persevere and do the will of God, we will receive what God promised (Hebrews 10:36). What are you expecting? The answer is on the way. Don't give up!

The Confession of Your Mouth: Do you have to see to believe or are you convinced God's promises are truth regardless of what you see? Do the words of your mouth confirm or destroy your faith? Your tongue is a powerful weapon that can bring death or bring life (Proverbs 18:21).

For example, if you believe you received healing from God, you weaken faith by talking about and magnifying your sickness. Instead of confessing your aches and pains, confess God's Word! His Word is the truth and it is the truth that sets you free. By the wounds of Jesus, you are healed (I Peter 2:24). Jesus took your sickness upon Himself at the cross (Matthew 8:17). Sickness and disease have no right to be in your body! It must bow to the name of Jesus, the Name above all names! That is the truth!

Confess the truth of the Bible and expect your faith confession to manifest. Let your words build faith instead of destroying faith. Be aware of the words you confess as you can be snared by the doubt-filled words of your mouth (Proverbs 6:2, NKJV).

Doubt squelches faith. In the natural we believe what we see, feel or experience. Our natural mind is very limited in assisting us with the development of faith. Faith must be based on God's Word, not on what our minds can comprehend. If faith goes no further than what we can reason in our mind, doubt will prevail every time.

We cannot expect anything from God if we doubt. "He who doubts is like a wave of the sea, blown and tossed by the wind. That man should not think he will receive anything from the Lord; he is a double-minded man, unstable in all he does" (James 1:6-8).

Doubt likes to creep into your mind when visible answers to prayer don't materialize within a preferred time frame. If answers to prayer are not coming fast enough for you, don't fall into the trap of confessing defeat. Words of doubt destroy faith and steal your blessings as well.

Resist doubt and remind yourself of the promises you initially based your prayer on. If doubt surfaces, confess the scriptures you are standing on. If God said it is His will – *it is His will* – you will see the answer come to pass as you stand in faith.

## FAITH FOR OTHERS HAS LIMITATIONS

You can have confidence that God's promises will be fulfilled in your own life when you pray in faith, yet your faith will not always work for other people. You can pray and pray until you are blue in the face for someone who needs healing in his body, yet he may remain sick. If he embraces unforgiveness in his heart or does not believe the God's Word as truth, your prayer of faith will not work unless, through God's grace and sovereignty, He performs the miracle anyway. Even if God does heal him through your prayer of faith, the one you prayed for eventually must stand on his own faith to maintain his healing.

All people possess a will of their own. Their choices affect God's ability to move on their behalf. God is always faithful to His Word, but each individual plays an important role in bringing God's promises to pass in his life.

You cannot rely on other people's faith to bring God's promises to pass in your life either. Although joining with others in prayer is a good practice, you shouldn't be dependent on others for your prayer needs. God expects you to grow in faith through study and practice of His Word. Each believer must develop the measure of faith he is given.

## PRAYING CONTINUALLY

Although you can receive your inheritance in Christ by faith, other areas of your life require continuous, never ceasing prayer. Praying for God's plan in your children's lives, your marriage, or career are just a few areas needing on-going prayer. Ask and ask and ask again. Keep knocking on God's door until you get the answer! (Luke 11:5-8). Desperate prayer moves the heart of God. Like Jacob, hold on and don't let go until you get the blessing! (Genesis 32:22-29)

God has a plan for your marriage, children and career, yet Satan's evil force continually aims flaming arrows attempting to destroy the plan of God. Praying once for your child's safety does not guarantee a lifetime of safety. Asking God for wisdom once does not guarantee an unending flow of wisdom for the rest of your life. Asking God once to help you on your job does not guarantee a trouble-free workplace forever. Keep your loved ones and the details of the plan for your life covered in prayer. Pray continually (1 Thessalonians 5:17).

## WISDOM FROM THE THRONE

God will direct the plan for your career, schooling, ministry, etc through a submitted life of prayer. God's wisdom and direction are needed for all aspects of your individual life not spelled out in Scripture. God promises to provide abundant wisdom when you ask for it (James 1:5). Receive wisdom by faith and then expect it! God brings wisdom through many avenues you may not expect.

Do you remember the story of the Israelites being deceived by the Gibeonites? (Joshua 9). After hearing the report of the destruction of Jericho, the Gibeonites planned a sneaky strategy in order to avoid suffering the same demise. The Gibeonites deceptively produced moldy bread and cracked wineskins to make it appear as if they had traveled from a distant land. Wanting to protect themselves, the Gibeonites slyly expressed a desire to make a treaty of peace with Israel.

Shortly after agreeing to a peace treaty, the Israelites realized that the Gibeonites had not come from afar but instead were actually their next door neighbors. They had been fooled! Why did the Israelites fall into the trap of deception? They were deceived because *they did not inquire of the Lord* (Joshua 9:14).

Do not underestimate the importance of asking God for wisdom. We must approach God for wisdom and direction in all areas of our lives or risk falling onto the wrong path. Receive a daily dose of Godly wisdom!

## ASK HIM!

God wants you to ask Him for what you need. Have you made your requests known to Him? Have you been specific? Is it possible you don't have what you need because you haven't asked?

Although God knows what you need before you ask, He instructs you continually to ask: "*Ask* and you will receive, and your joy will be complete" (John 16:24); "Whatever you *ask* for in prayer, believe that you have received it, and it will be yours" (Mark 11:24); "You do not have, because you do not *ask God*" (James 4:2); "*Ask* and it will be given to you; seek and you will find; knock and the door will be opened to you. For everyone who *asks* receives; he who seeks finds; and to him who knocks, the door will be opened" (Matthew 7:7-8). God made it clear: Ask Him!

## WHY AREN'T MY PRAYERS GETTING ANSWERED?

What if prayers seem to go unanswered? If you sense your prayers are falling on deaf ears, consider examining these areas:

Unforgiveness: If you harbor unforgiveness in your heart, your prayers will definitely be hindered. Jesus said, "When you stand praying, if you hold anything against anyone, forgive him, so that your Father in heaven may forgive you your sins" (Mark 11:25). This verse follows Mark 11:24, which is the assurance that if you believe you received a promise of God you can know you will have it. Praise God, this is good news – great news! But you cannot ignore the command to forgive in Mark 11:25 as you stand in faith because faith and forgiveness are dependent on one another.

The sin of unforgiveness blocks your prayers to God and causes Him to have a deaf ear. Sin causes God to hide His face from you (Isaiah 59:2). Unforgivenss is sin! If you forgive others, God forgives you but if you will not forgive others, God will not forgive you (Matthew 6:14-15). If you hold a grudge against anyone, your sins are piling up against you. You cannot have God's ear if your heart is full of the cancer of unforgiveness. Choose to lay it down at the cross.

Wrong Motivation: Another area to check when you lack answers to prayer is the motivation of your heart when you pray. Are your motives pure? Your prayer request will most likely not come to pass until your motives are in line with God's heartbeat. Take the time to search your heart and examine the motivation behind the petitions you bring before God in prayer. You will not receive from God when your motives are wrong (James 4:3). Are your motives selfish or prideful or are your motives pure in fulfilling God's plan and purpose?

Have You Done Your Part?: If frustrated with unanswered prayer, ask yourself if you have done your part. For example, if you're standing in faith for employment, are you sending out resumes and following up on them? Are you making phone calls and diligently knocking on doors? If you're lounging on the couch, watching television and eating bonbons day after day, don't be surprised if a job doesn't fall from heaven into your lap. You haven't done your part!

Often out of ignorance, believers ask God to move on their behalf and then proceed to sit back and relax as they wait for God to perform a miracle. "I'm waiting on God" is a common Christian excuse. Could God be waiting for you to do your part? Take steps of faith and get moving in some direction. God will step in to finish the rest.

God's Timing Is Not Your Timing: God's timing is simply not always your timing. Exercise patience as you continue to stand in faith for answers to your petitions. Waiting on the Lord creates an opportunity to develop maturity in patience. Wait with an expectant heart though, not a doubting heart.

Perseverance in prayer is necessary especially as we pray for salvation of unbelievers. How glorious it would be if we prayed for the salvation of our loved ones one day and saw them saved the next day. That's rarely the case though. It often requires years of expectant prayer before a loved one chooses to accept Jesus as Lord and Savior.

What a heavenly day of rejoicing it is when those loved ones get saved! You need to persevere! Keep the switch of faith turned on regardless of how long you wait for the answer to your heartfelt prayer. Do not turn faith off under any circumstances but instead pray with expectation and trust God's perfect timing!

God Knows More Than We Do: If you pray in faith according to the God's Word, yet your petition does not come to pass, it is easy to cry, "Why, God?" Believers often question God when prayers do not get answered in the way they feel they should be answered. The reason you do not get the answers you expect is never an indication that God missed it somewhere, changed His mind or made an error in His revealed will. God never makes mistakes.

I once prayed for a man who was on life support and near death. Following God's instruction to lay hands on the sick in Jesus' Name (Mark 16:15-18), I laid hands on this sick man and prayed in faith for his healing. I fully expected him to recover, yet he died two days later.

Why did the man die? God did not reveal the reason to me, but the truth of the Word of God still reveals His provision for our health and His desire for us to lay hands on the sick. Because the man died when I expected him to live does not change God's Word.

Maybe you have prayed for someone who died as well. Although you will not always understand the outcome of your prayers, you must allow God to be God and choose to continue to trust Him. Continue to obey God's revealed Word even if you do not understand. You cannot lean on your own understanding but must simply trust that God is in control (Proverbs 3:5). God sees the big picture, we don't.

Do Not Be Anxious: Are you praying about your cares and concerns and then worrying about them? Is anxiety keeping you awake at night? God does not want you to carry the burden of your trials. He wants to carry them for you. Cast your cares on the Lord, and leave them there (1 Peter 5:7). Don't take them back! Resist the temptation to pick up what you've already laid down.

Can you trust God with your cares? Can you trust God for the victory? You may not see the victory from where you stand, but God can. Praise God, you can be free from worry and anxiety after you leave your concerns at the feet of Jesus! He cares about you and knows every detail of every situation in your life. The issues of your life, both big and small, matter to God.

The peace of God envelops and guards you as you obey His instruction in Philippians 4:6-7. "Do not be anxious about anything, but in everything, by prayer and petition, with thanksgiving, present your requests to God. And the peace of God, which transcends all understanding, will guard your hearts and your minds in Christ Jesus." Do not be anxious about *anything*. God wants *all* of your cares. If you feel anxious and fretful, go back to the cross and leave your cares with Jesus.

God promises to keep you in perfect peace when your mind is stayed on Him because you trust in Him (Isaiah 26:3, NKJV). Is your mind stayed on Him? Are you trusting in Him or are you having an anxiety attack?

### FELLOWSHIP WITH GOD IN THE MIDST OF TRIALS
God desires fellowship with you whether you are in a mountaintop experience or in the valley of trial. Does your attitude toward God change when circumstances change? Is your prayer life abundant and fruitful in the midst of victory and dry or nonexistent during turmoil? Do you give God thanksgiving and praise only when things go well? God is worthy of praise and glory and honor at all times. Do you want to locate your spiritual maturity? Examine yourself in the midst

of your trials.

Consider Paul and Silas' example of faithful prayer in the midst of tremendous trial (Acts 16:22-26). While faithfully serving God, Paul and Silas were attacked, stripped, beaten and thrown into an inner prison cell with their feet fastened in stocks.

What was their response? At midnight, they prayed and sang hymns to God! What was God's response? A violent earthquake shook the foundations of the prison, the prison doors flew open, and everybody's chains came loose.

What a midnight for Paul and Silas! While serving God with all of their heart, soul and strength, Paul and Silas were beaten and tossed into a damp jail. Did they whine and complain about the unfairness of their trial by saying, "What's going on, Lord? We faithfully served You. We've brought glory to Your Name and this is what we get in return? What's up with this?" No, Paul and Silas prayed and sang hymns to God. Their less than desirable circumstances did not hinder their prayer life. They pushed right through to the victory. Their prayer and praise broke their bondage and ushered in the victory.

What is your attitude in the midst of a midnight experience? What does your attitude reflect in the dark times of your life? Choose to praise God like never before. Offer up a sacrifice of praise in the midst of your trial and see God shake the foundations of your prison to usher in the victory!

## BE FILLED WITH THE HOLY SPIRIT

No doubt, being born into the kingdom of God is the most tremendous blessing of life. Forgiven and cleansed of sin, you have a future eternity with your heavenly Father, praise the Lord! God has even more for you though! God desires to fill you with His precious Holy Spirit. He wants to help you right now on earth.

Being filled with the Holy Spirit is an experience separate from the new birth. We see examples of the believers in Samaria (Acts 8:14-17) and the believers in Ephesus (Acts 19:1-7)) many years after the day of Pentecost who were born again, yet had not received the Holy Spirit.

I, like those believers, was born again and water baptized, yet did not realize God had even more for me. Although the Holy Spirit dwelled within me since the day I was born again, He did not have complete control until I surrendered to Him wholly. When God filled me with His Spirit with the evidence of speaking in tongues, I developed a deeper and more intimate communion with God in prayer. The power of God is released through the Holy Spirit (Acts 1:8).

God will fill you and empower you with His Spirit as well. Have you asked Him? He always gives to those who ask. Luke 11:11-13 assures us of God's willingness to give us His Spirit: "Which of you fathers, if your son asks for a fish, will give him a snake instead? Or if he asks for an egg, will give him a scorpion? If you then, though you are evil, know how to give good gifts to your children, how much more will your Father in heaven give the Holy Spirit to those who ask him." Ask and you will receive!

One of the many benefits the Holy Spirit brings is to help you pray. When you pray in the Spirit, you will not understand what you are praying as the Spirit gives you the utterance (1 Corinthians 14:14). No one will understand you as you utter mysteries with your spirit (1 Corinthians 14:2). Christian friend, you cannot reason this truth out with your mind. Do not let your mind get in the way of receiving the blessing of the Spirit. You cannot reason out the mysteries of God.

Speaking in tongues is not a one-time occurrence that takes place when you receive the Holy Spirit. You benefit greatly by praying in the Spirit as a regular part of your pray life. Praying in the Holy Spirit reminds you of His indwelling presence (1 Corinthians 3:16). Get a daily filling of God's Spirit.

You can rely on the precious Holy Spirit to help you pray about situations you are not certain how to pray about or do not fully understand. He intercedes for you according to God's will, not according to your will or understanding (Romans 8:26-27). Hallelujah! Let the Holy Spirit intercede for you when you pray. You pray unselfishly when you pray in the Spirit because you pray according to God's plan instead of your plan.

## RESIST BONDAGE IN PRAYER

When I first established a prayer life, I developed a legalistic prayer ritual. I read the Bible from 5-5:30 a.m. sharp, offered a time of praise and thanksgiving, then prayed for specific things in a specific order. At 7:00 sharp my prayer time ended. If I started late or if my children interrupted my prayer, I felt guilty and attempted to make up the lost time during the day. Quickly realizing my time with the Lord was ineffective and dry, God's grace led me to understand His desire for a much more fulfilling and intimate time of fellowship, not a legalistic prayer ritual.

I was pleasantly surprised to learn that I could talk to God throughout the day, not only in my prayer closet. Do you leave God behind when you leave your prayer closet? You have the great privilege of enjoying communion with God throughout the day. Wherever you are at the moment can be a place of prayer and fellowship with God. God does not live in your prayer closet. He lives within you!

Allow the Holy Spirit to lead you in prayer instead of following a legalistic prayer ritual, as I did. Your prayer life may differ greatly from day to day as you follow the leading of the Holy Spirit. If you pray two hours one day and fifteen minutes the next, God will not condemn you! If you spend a majority of your prayer time in praise and worship one day and focus on bringing requests before the Lord the next, it's perfectly fine! Do not put God in a box. Let Him lead as you find freedom and liberty in the presence of God.

## GET QUIET BEFORE GOD

As you spend time in God's presence, allow Him to speak to your heart. You don't need to do all of the talking. Listen to the voice of the Spirit. The Spirit of truth will guide you into all truth and will speak only what he hears from the Father (John 16:13). Be still and listen intently, as His voice is often a gentle whisper.

Some of my most precious times with the Lord are spent sitting quietly in His presence. I'm on the go continually, surrounded with the clamor of a busy and quick moving schedule, so I've had to learn to get quiet before God. For me, meeting with God is best early in the morning, before the kids arise, before the hustle bustle starts, before the phone rings. What about you? Is there a special time or place you meet with God?

Quieting our mind, body and soul prepares a platform for the Spirit of God to speak. When we settle ourselves, we can hear the often soft whisper of the Spirit of God.

Listen to the still, small voice of the Spirit. Go to your secret place with God and get quiet before Him. This does not mean, however, that you should listen for audible voices. You tread dangerous ground by seeking voices; Satan is more than willing to accommodate you if it is voices you want to hear. Although God has spoken audibly to some, it is rare. Let God speak to you in the way He chooses. Don't forget, God talks to you every day through the Bible. It's His personal Word to you.

Beware! There should be a flashing danger signal if you sense God spoke something that does not line up with His Word. God will not contradict Himself. For example, if you are married and feel God wants you to divorce your spouse so you can be with someone else, you better get in God's presence and get your heart right. You didn't hear from God!

Many well-meaning Christians get off into left field as they put their faith in voices, dreams, visions, or false prophecies contradicting the truth of God's Word. Voices, dreams, visions or prophecies should never be elevated above the Word of God. Mass destruction can take place when we get outside the Word of God. If *anything* does not line up with Scripture, it's simply not from God. God will *never* tell you to do something that contradicts His Word. *Never.*

## GOD IS WAITING FOR YOU

A tremendous privilege awaits you in the throne room. The God of the universe desires intimate time with you. Have you made a daily appointment to meet with God? His schedule is flexible enough to accommodate any time you choose.

In that quiet place of your choice, meet with God. You will be changed after meeting with the King as His presence transforms you and His sweet fragrance lingers throughout the day.

The King of Kings and Lord of Lords awaits you. Touch His

throne of grace as you enter into the Holy of Holies through the blood of the lamb. Enter, child of God, the King awaits you.

# CHAPTER 12
## Serving The Master

### GOD HAS A PLAN FOR YOUR LIFE

God rescued you from the dominion of darkness and translated you into His kingdom (Colossians 1:13) with a destiny. God placed you in the body of Christ with a purpose and a plan to carry out His divine will on the earth. Long before you were born, God customized a plan for you and you alone. No one else can fulfill your destiny, as it was tailor-made for you by God Himself.

### THE BODY OF CHRIST

Jesus is the head of the church and we are His body (Colossians 1:18). Each individual part of the body of Christ is significant; no part is more important than another nor is one position superior to another. Because each part has a purpose, each must fulfill his part in the body of Christ so the body functions the way God intended it to function.

How would the physical body function without a right arm? – without eyes? – without ears? All parts fulfill a specific purpose necessary for the body to function properly. Paul talks about the physical body consisting of many parts functioning together in 1 Corinthians 12:14-20:

Now the body is not made up of one part but of many. If the foot should say, "Because I am not a hand, I do not belong to the body," it would not for that reason cease to be part of the body. And if the ear should say, "Because I am not an eye, I do not belong to the body," it would not for that reason cease to be part of the body. If the whole body were an eye, where would the sense of hearing be? If the whole body were an ear,

171

where would the sense of smell be? But in fact God has arranged the parts in the body, every one of them, just as he wanted them to be. If they were all one part, where would the body be? As it is, there are many parts, but one body.

How interesting the physical body would look and operate if all parts were the same. If made up of only eyes, the body would enjoy excellent vision, however could not walk, talk, eat or feel. It would miss out on a multitude of critical parts necessary to perform effectively.

In the same way, the body of Christ would not operate properly if all members had the same function. If all were teachers, the body would be full of knowledge, but who would oversee the flock? Who would care for the children? Who would usher in the presence of God through praise and worship?

God placed many different parts in His body, each one critical to the fulfillment of His plan and purpose. There is place – *a significant place* – for each member of the body of Christ.

## GOD PLACED DIFFERENT GIFTS IN THE BODY

Each believer has his own gift from God (1 Corinthians 7:7). God placed both natural and spiritual gifts within each member of the body of Christ, not leaving anyone out. The Apostle Paul speaks of the importance of each person operating in the gifts God gave him: "We have different gifts, according to the grace given us. If a man's gift is prophesying, let him use it in proportion to his faith. If it is serving, let him serve; if it is teaching, let him teach; if it is encouraging, let him encourage; if it is contributing to the needs of others, let him give generously; if it is leadership, let him govern diligently; if it is showing mercy, let him do it cheerfully" (Romans 12:4-8).

Every believer is placed in the body of Christ equipped with gifts to fulfill an important purpose – *God's purpose*. Each part of the body was created with a God-ordained function.

What if the eye suddenly decided it would rather be a hand? What if the mouth no longer wanted to be a mouth but instead desired to be a foot? It simply wouldn't work because the eye and mouth cannot operate in the function intended for the hand and foot.

Some believers covet other people's God-given gifts instead of operating in their own gifts. One cannot operate in another person's gift any easier than a physical body part can operate as another body part.

A musician in our church sings with an angelic voice. How the heavens open as she leads us into the presence of God through praise and worship! God's presence fills the sanctuary when she sings. What if I were not satisfied with the gifts God gave me and coveted her gift instead? If I tried to function in her gift, it would not be pleasant to the ear by any stretch of the imagination! I may be capable of making a joyful noise unto the Lord but I could not operate in her gift, as God did not anoint me to sing. He anointed her though, and praise God, she brings glory to His Name as she flows in her gift.

The flip side is true as well. This talented musician could not step into the gifts God anointed me for as those gifts were designed for me to fulfill the destiny God planned for my life.

How will God's plan and purpose for your life be fulfilled if you try to fulfill someone else's destiny? Are you operating in your gift or trying to operate in someone else's gift? Avoid coveting other people's gifts. Cherish the gifts God gave you.

Watch your destiny unfold as you seek God for the release and stirring of your gifts. Take time to discover the gifts God placed on the inside of you. Do you realize the critical part you play in God's divine plan? Are you ready to discover the gifts God anointed you with? Are you ready to serve the Master?

## MUCH IS REQUIRED OF THOSE WHO ARE GIVEN MUCH

I talked to a man once who admired the ministry of one of the great evangelists of our day. He commented on the stadiums full of people that gathered to hear him preach God's Word. I wondered if the man realized the great price this evangelist likely paid in answering God's call to ministry. Yes, God equipped the evangelist to do great things for the kingdom of God but also required much of him in order to fulfill the call to ministry. If one knew the evangelist personally, he would likely discover that he sacrificed much to do God's work.

The Bible says, "From everyone who has been given much, much will be demanded and from the one who has been entrusted with much, much more will be asked" (Luke 12:48). The more God gives you, the more you will be accountable for, therefore you must take care to steward over the God's gifts. Are you willing to pay the price to fulfill God's call?

## SOWING YOUR TIME AND TALENTS

Being spiritually challenged by God's Word and enjoying Christian fellowship on a regular basis is critical. One claiming, "I don't need to attend church to serve or love God," deceives himself. Isolating yourself from the rest of the body causes you to miss out on God's divine plan for His Church. The Apostle Paul writes, "Let us not give up meeting together, as some are in the habit of doing, but let us encourage one another – and all the more as you see the Day approaching" (Hebrews 10:25). The body cannot function if the parts are isolated from each other.

Being part of the body of Christ is much more than simply attending church on Sunday morning. God reserved a special place for you in His body and needs you and the gifts He gave you to accomplish His will on the earth. King David tells us, "The righteous will flourish like a palm tree. They will grow like a cedar of Lebanon planted in the house of our God" (Psalm 92:12-13). Get planted in God's house! You need to put your roots down in order to grow.

In churches today, twenty percent of the people typically do eighty percent of the work. People offer many excuses for not contributing their time and talent to serve in the church: "I'm getting fed right now"; "I'm receiving my spiritual filling"; "The responsibilities in the church don't meet my schedule"; "I don't have anything to offer"; "Someone else can do the job better than me"; "I'm too busy"; "I don't think there's a place for me."

Do you confess any of these excuses or maybe others? Your service is vital. We all need to serve – every one of us – in order to fulfill the purpose of God's Church.

Because many are unwilling to fill positions needed in the church, the burden of responsibility is left to the ones who step forward to fill the gap. This overburden can result in some becoming burnt-out and out of balance. When people step forward only because nobody else is willing, they often fill positions God never intended them to fill.

Families, marriages and children suffer when Christians are overburdened by filling more positions than God called them to. It is possible to be involved in many fruitful activities in the church, yet at the same time have a personal life out of balance. It is not God's plan for you or your family to be out of balance. If Christians seek God's direction for guidance to the places He gifted them for, the church can run like a well-oiled engine, forging ahead full of energy and joy.

God did not intend for your gifts to remain dormant but instead wants you to use your gift to serve others and to faithfully administer God's grace (1 Peter 4:10). What did God call you to do? You may have tremendous gifts lying dormant inside of you. Lives are waiting to be touched with your gift. Submit yourself to God; stir up that gift and let God draw it out of you.

Christians can become spiritually fat by keeping God's gifts to themselves. Too many believers attend church week after week only to receive. They get filled up on spiritual food, yet are unwilling to pour out what they receive. The fatter they get, the more stagnant and dry they become. Are you self-serving or surrendered to God for His service? Freely you have received; freely give (Romans 3:24).

Continually fill yourself with God's precious Holy Spirit and bless others by pouring out what you received. Streams of living water – the Holy Spirit – will flow *from you* (John 7:37-38). Hallelujah! Empty yourself out to God and ask Him to fill you to overflowing with His Spirit. When full of the Holy Spirit, you naturally want to serve.

## ARE YOU WAITING ON GOD OR IS HE WAITING ON YOU?

How common for a believer to wait on God for direction in servitude while at the same time, God is waiting on him!

When the Lord moved our family to Eastern Washington, we prayed and diligently sought God for direction in our new church home. We submitted ourselves to God and were willing to do anything He asked of us.

After four months of dedicated prayer, silence rang from the heavens. We heard nothing! Instead of waiting for a neon light to illuminate a flashing signal from heaven, we met with our pastor and made ourselves available to be used wherever the greatest need existed.

We spent several months serving in various capacities, all of which we knew were not our "calling." As we began serving though, God began to direct our path. As we moved, God moved. Increasing focus came to our purpose as we served the Master and submitted ourselves to His plan.

Many Christians want to serve, yet are not sure where God is trying to lead them. If you lack clear direction, step out and serve wherever you can. *Do something.* Proverbs 16:9 says, "In his heart a man plans his course, but the Lord determines his steps."

Have you planned your course? Once you start moving, God will guide your steps. God will lead you where He wants you to be – but you first need to move in some direction. He can't direct you if you're standing still!

There may be areas in the church you feel drawn to, yet a gnawing feeling of inadequacy or fear holds you back from stepping out and getting your feet wet. Fear not! God will fill your inability with His ability. When you step out, God steps in!

When stepping out in faith, even in areas you feel you are not called to or gifted in, you may be surprised to discover that God wants to use you in the very area you felt inadequate. How will you know if you don't try? Have you left the starting gate? The door is open!

Opportunities to serve in the church are endless. Caring for babies, welcoming visitors, teaching children, preparing meals, visiting the sick, and interceding in prayer are just a few of the opportunities available to serve. Whether you have served God for twenty years or for one day, God has prepared a place for you. Needs exist in the body of Christ right now. Are you willing to fulfill those needs?

Are you waiting for God to reveal the perfect job for you? Maybe God is waiting on you. Imagine how silly it would be to sit in your car, turning the steering wheel this way and that way. *Hmmm, why aren't I getting anywhere?* You obviously will not get anywhere until you start the engine, put it in gear and get moving! Likewise, when you start moving in service to God, He will direct you.

## GET OUT OF THE COMFORT ZONE

God delights in placing us in positions that are rather uncomfortable. Stretching us beyond our limited human ability and strength helps us realize our complete dependence on Him. Don't miss your calling because it's bigger than you are. When you stretch yourself and push out self-made limitations, God molds you into the person He created you to be. God will do miracles in your life… if you allow Him to.

Do you want to grow? Step out of your comfort zone where spiritual growth and maturity abound. Be strong and courageous! Get out of the boat – step out on the water. You'll find Jesus waiting there with open arms.

Tom once faced a unique opportunity to be spiritually stretched when he was asked to lead both a prayer ministry and an usher ministry. Both positions required a significant amount of commitment and time. Tom is naturally gifted with management and leadership skills so overseeing the usher ministry would have been a natural fit for him. As he prayed though, the Holy Spirit prodded him to lead the prayer ministry, a place far out of his comfort zone. Although this was new territory for Tom, he obeyed God's leading.

Tom's season in the prayer ministry produced a bumper crop of fruitful spiritual growth. He found victory, as he trusted God to equip him to serve with excellence. Be bold and resist taking the easy, comfy jobs. Let God stretch you in places where you must cling to Him for the victory.

## OVERCOMING THE GIANT OF FEAR

Fear hinders many Christians from fulfilling their destiny in Christ. Is fear hindering you? Are you afraid of failure or leery of looking foolish? Does the idea of serving in a new area scare you? Do you fear that potential success will lead you through new doors of opportunity that you may not want to go through?

Gripping fear can hinder the fulfillment of God's plan for your life. Fear must be dealt with head on, or it will squelch your destiny and cause God's gifts to lie dormant. God did not send the giant of fear (2 Timothy 1:7) but He will help you conquer it.

I was once asked to develop and teach a new adult Sunday school class. The idea petrified me, yet I knew God had opened a divine door that I had to step through. *Oh God, I can't do it!* I thought. *I'm too scared! What if I fail? What if I make a mistake? How am I going to do this?* Stepping through the door of obedience, I stood face to face with the giant of fear and entered a time of expanding my self-made limitations.

Although I hoped God would graciously allow me to get broken in with a small class, I did not get my way. Not only did the registration sheet continue to grow, the attendees included several pastors. *Yikes!* I thought, feeling butterflies flutter around in my nervous stomach. *Oh God, I'm so scared.* Acknowledging my complete dependence, I said, *God, I can't do this without you.*

After bathing the class in prayer, I studied and prepared myself for the first lesson. Sensing God's direction, He taught me to trust in Him instead of trusting in my own natural ability. Confident that God opened this door, I knew He equipped me to accomplish what He asked of me. Strengthened by the power of God, I was determined and prepared to face my giant.

A nervous stomach and knocking knees accompanied me to the first class. As I shakily stepped to the front and began teaching though, God showed up. As the weeks passed, greater excitement and confidence enveloped me; I could hardly wait for class to share the fresh revelation God breathed into the lessons.

Fear vanished and the franticly fluttering butterflies no longer made their home in my stomach. My knees no longer shook. Praise God, my giant of fear was nowhere to be seen! God faithfully helped break the bondage of fear by leading me to a place I could face and conquer the giant that lurked in my life.

The most effective way to overcome fear is to face it head on and step right through it. In the story of David and Goliath (1 Samuel 17) we see David, only a boy, facing a tremendous challenge from the obnoxious giant. As Goliath, over nine feet tall, moved closer to attack David, David did not turn and run away. Instead he ran quickly *toward* the battle line to meet him. Aggressively facing his giant Goliath, he conquered his giant in the strength of the Lord.

Do not run from fear. Confront it! When fear says, "You can't do it… you'll never make it… you'll fail if you try," say, "Yes, I can do it and I will do it!" I can do *all* things through Christ who strengthens me! (Philippians 4:13). It doesn't sound very easy, does it? It's not easy to face fears. Rarely will God ask you to do the easy thing but if you rely on God for strength you can overcome any fear *through Him.*

Determination to fulfill God's purpose enables you to step through fear by faith – knees knocking and all. If God gives you an assignment and your knees are knocking – I challenge you to do it with your knees knocking! If your stomach is nervous, do it with a nervous stomach! Face your fears and find the victory that comes only through God. Your Christian journey will forge ahead when you determine to conquer the giant of fear. Don't let fear hold you back!

## SERVING THE KING IN EXCELLENCE

When God opens a door for you to serve in the body of Christ, do everything you can in the natural to accomplish what He asked of you. Only a fool expects God's miraculous intervention if he's been irresponsible and unfaithful in doing his part. What if I showed up to teach my class without preparing, studying, or praying? What if I said, "Well God, it's up to you, I trust you to help me teach." I would have faced disaster.

If God placed you in a position of teaching Sunday School, did you spend time in prayer, prepare yourself with the lessons, and develop a plan for your class? If you are an usher, are you familiar with the expectations? Do you arrive on time for services and meetings? God equips you for everything He calls you to do but you also play an important part in getting the job done. Be faithful in doing your part.

What would happen if you arrived late for work on a regular basis? What if you had a presentation to give at the office and decided not to show up because you were too tired that day? It would only be a matter of time before you were unemployed.

If you strive to demonstrate excellence in the workplace, how much more excellence should be demonstrated in the body of Christ! Are you treating your service in the church as a privilege? You are serving the King of Kings! The King deserves excellence in your service to Him.

## PREPARATION FOR MINISTRY

God puts you through a proving ground to prepare you for other positions He plans for you. You must be willing and faithful in doing the small things before He will trust you with bigger things.

Joseph was not elevated to ruler of Egypt immediately (Genesis 37-50). He experienced well over 20 years of preparation. He served Potiphar, spent several years in prison, interpreted dreams, and faithfully accomplished many other tasks, both pleasant and unpleasant, as God prepared him. The dream God gave Joseph as a teenager didn't come to pass until he was a grown man. What patience he demonstrated!

Joseph did not complain his way through those years of preparation, but instead matured and grew through each place God led him. Joseph squeezed everything he could out of each experience he walked through. Are you willing to submit to your preparation time? Are you willing to squeeze all you can out of each place God leads you?

King David was not crowned King of Israel overnight either (1 Samuel 16-2 Samuel 5). David tended sheep before he killed a lion. Conquering the lion prepared him for killing a bear. Killing a bear prepared David for killing Goliath. Killing Goliath prepared him for killing ten thousands. Killing ten thousands prepared him for being King. All were part of God's ultimate plan for David; all were stepping-stones to David's destiny. Just as with Joseph, much of David's preparation was accomplished through God-ordained seasons of trial where he learned to be a selfless servant of the Most High.

You will also have a time of preparation for service to the King of Kings. Are you called to full time ministry? Maybe you're called to be a pastor or an evangelist. A time of preparation is necessary for all things. A believer does not get born again one day and the next day print business cards with "Pastor" under his name. He must first put one foot in front of the other and endure God's time of preparation.

Sometimes a new believer, out of his zeal for the Lord, wants God to take him from point A to point Z overnight. The reality is, however, that you must go through point A to get to point B and then progress from point B to point C. At each step along the way, if you remain teachable, you grow and mature while God prepares you to move on. I suspect if God gave you a glimpse of what awaited you at point Z you would be petrified, as you simply would not be prepared for it. God prepares your destiny through divine, on-going on the job training.

Let God decide when it's time for promotion. You do not graduate from college immediately following kindergarten but instead grow and mature over time. You grow and mature spiritually over time as well. Don't be in a rush to move on. Learn all you can at the place God has you. He will move you on in His perfect time.

## SERVING GOD IS NOT
## A CONVENIENT PART TIME POSITION

Be sensitive for opportunities to be used as God's servant – both inside and outside the walls of the church. Serving God is not limited to the four walls of the church building on Sunday mornings. Wherever you set foot is an opportunity to do God's work. When God has a job to get done, are you prepared to step forward?

When asked to assist with an activity that inconveniences your schedule, are you willing or do you serve only when it meets your schedule or preference? A humble servant is available to the King 24 hours a day. Christians must understand a key truth that is often ignored: *A servant of the Most High does not live a life of convenience.*

## SERVE AS UNTO THE LORD

As you submit yourself to God for His service, your work may appear to go unnoticed by man. Have you ever invested a tremendous amount of time and energy into something, yet got no recognition whatsoever? Don't worry. God saw it. God sees *everything* you do. In all service, serve with all your heart, as if you are serving the Lord, not man (Ephesians 6:7). Remember whom you serve.

Paul writes in Colossians 3:23-24, "Whatever you do, work at it with all your heart, as working for the Lord, not for men, since you know that you will receive an inheritance from the Lord as a reward. It is the Lord Christ you are serving." Your reward comes from the Almighty, not from man.

Serving God in areas that seem to go unnoticed trains you to become selfless in your service to Him. Many miss out on the great opportunities God prepared for them because of an unwillingness to become a servant; they are unwilling to do the jobs they get no recognition for. Learning to be a servant, *a selfless servant*, produces a victorious and fruitful Christian.

I once met an eager Bible school student. Upon graduation, he immediately printed his ministry cards and aggressively sought a ministry position. He was offered the opportunity to care for the children, clean the church and serve in other areas of need, but was unwilling. These positions were too menial to him and did not offer him the recognition he sought. Because there were no prominent ministry positions available for him at the time, he got angry and left the church.

Crossing paths with him several years later, I found him spiritually stagnant, not serving God or even attending church. Why? He was unwilling to learn the most critical part of ministry preparation: Becoming a selfless servant of the Most High.

If you are faithful with the little things God gives you, He will promote you. God rewards faithfulness, not titles or positions. Whether you clean toilets or preach to multitudes, do it faithfully with a servant's heart.

## DO A CHECK UP ON YOUR MOTIVES

While searching for areas to serve in the body of Christ, examine your motives. Why do you want to get involved in the ministry you are considering? If your motive is to obtain recognition for yourself or to receive praise from man, your motives are wrong and your service will be short-lived and worthless in God's sight. If your motive is to please God, to glorify His Name and to fulfill His divine plan and purpose, your service will endure and produce everlasting fruit. God sees what you do and knows the motives of your heart (Proverbs 16:2).

Elevating yourself before man in service to God is a grave mistake. But if you come before God as a humble servant, willing to do whatever He asks of you, He will lift you up. If you exalt yourself, you will be humbled, but if you humble yourself, you will be exalted (Luke 14:11). Let God lift you up.

## TO BE LIKE JESUS IS TO BE A SERVANT

As a born again believer, you are predestined to be conformed to the image of Jesus, therefore you are predestined to be a servant! Paul shares in Philippians 2:6-8, "Who, being in very nature God, did not consider equality with God something to be grasped, but made himself nothing, taking the very nature of a servant, being made in human likeness. And being found in appearance as a man, he humbled himself and became obedient to death – even to death on a cross!"

My precious Grandma Ruth often told me, "Honey, we were saved to serve." Yes, child of God, you too were saved to serve. The Lord Jesus Christ humbled Himself and served all the way to the cross. Are you willing to humble yourself to serve the Master?

How glorious it will be as you complete your journey in Christ on this earth, meet Him face to face and hear, "Well done, good and faithful servant! You have been faithful with a few things; I will put you in charge of many things. Come and share your master's happiness" (Matthew 25: 23).

## CONCLUSION

We've almost completed a soul-stirring journey through the pages of this book. On your travels through the truth of the Word of God, I hope you've found heart-swelling joy in discovering your inheritance in Christ. You've also likely been challenged to examine areas of your life that had yet to be surrendered to the perfect will of God.

Knowing your inheritance in Christ and living according to God's

Word in full surrender to Him is a sure recipe for a fruitful Christian life. As you leave this book behind, I encourage you to take that recipe with you.

I trust you've soaked in some quiet moments to ponder the God-inspired words spilled onto each page and the scriptural truths peppered throughout each chapter. I've openly shared my personal challenges, miserable failures and great victories I've found through Christ Jesus and hope you've discovered through my testimony that you're not alone on your Christian journey. God holds your hand on a *life-long* journey of growth in Christ; a journey that is walked out day by day. It's my heart-felt prayer that *Breaking Out* provoked and inspired you to press on to complete your Christian journey in victory.

Because we've only touched on a small slice of God's truths, I exhort you to spend time daily in prayer and in study of His Holy Word to become fully persuaded of God's perfect will for your life. Daily He will walk with you up the mountains of victory and daily He will hold you up through the valleys of trial.

The Christian journey? It truly is a life-long journey. It began when you invited Christ into your heart and will not be complete until you take your last breath and enter into eternal glory. God has raised you up for such a time as this, friend in Christ. In this day and in this hour, you will fulfil your God-ordained destiny by walking hand in hand with God the Father, God the Son and God the Holy Spirit.

May the God of hope fill you with all joy and peace as you trust in Him so that you will overflow with hope by the power of the Holy Spirit. I pray that God's finest blessings will be poured into your life as you continue your journey in Christ not only as His disciple, but as a co-laborer to make disciples of the nations.

*